The Paradox
of Subjectivity

The Paradox
of Subjectivity

THE SELF IN THE
TRANSCENDENTAL TRADITION

David Carr

New York   Oxford

Oxford University Press

1999

Oxford University Press

Oxford   New York
Athens   Auckland   Bangkok   Bogotá   Buenos Aires   Calcutta
Cape Town   Chennai   Dar es Salaam   Delhi   Florence   Hong Kong   Istanbul
Karachi   Kuala Lumpur   Madrid   Melbourne   Mexico City   Mumbai
Nairobi   Paris   São Paulo   Singapore   Taipei   Tokyo   Toronto   Warsaw

and associated companies in
Berlin   Ibadan

Published by Oxford University Press, Inc.
198 Madison Avenue, New York, New York 10016

Oxford is a registered trademark of Oxford University Press

Library of Congress Cataloging-in-Publication Data
Carr, David, 1940–
The paradox of subjectivity : the self in the
transcendental tradition / David Carr.
p.   cm.
Includes bibliographical references and index.
ISBN 0-19-512690-4
1. Self (Philosophy)   2. Transcendentalism.   3. Kant, Immanuel,
1724–1804.   4. Husserl, Edmund, 1859–1938.   I. Title.
BD438.5.C35   1998
126—dc21   98-28135

1 3 5 7 9 8 6 4 2

Printed in the United States of America
on acid-free paper

For Stefanie

Acknowledgments

In the earliest stages of this project I had the benefit of a released time grant from the Social Sciences and Humanities Research Council of Canada. The intermediate stages were greatly aided by the students in my graduate seminars at Emory University, where many of the ideas in this book were presented and discussed. In the final stages, Marc Lucht and Rudolf Makkreel read parts of the manuscript and provided helpful comments and suggestions. Thanks are also due to Edward Casey and Edward Dimendberg for their encouragement and support.

I am deeply indebted to my wife, Stefanie Graef Carr, for making it possible for me to complete this project, and for much more than that. I express my gratitude by dedicating this book to her.

Contents

Key to Abbreviations

Works by Edmund Husserl

CM = *Cartesian Meditations: An Introduction to Phenomenology*, tr. Dorion Cairns (The Hague: Martinus Nijhoff, 1960)

CR = *The Crisis of European Sciences and Transcendental Phenomenology: An Introduction to Phenomenological Philosophy*, tr. David Carr (Evanston: Northwestern University Press, 1970)

ID1 = *Ideas Pertaining to a Pure Phenomenology and to a Phenomenological Philosophy*. First Book, tr. F. Kersten (The Hague: Martinus Nijhoff, 1983)

ID2 = *Ideas Pertaining to a Pure Phenomenology and to a Phenomenological Philosophy*. Second Book, tr. R. Rojcewicz and A. Schuwer (The Hague: Martinus Nijhoff, 1989)

LI = *Logical Investigations,* tr. J. N. Findlay (New York: Humanities Press, 1970)

Works by Martin Heidegger

EP = "Das Ende der Philosophie und die Aufgabe des Denkens," in *Zur Sache des Denkens* (Tübingen: Max Niemeyer Verlag, 1969), pp. 61ff.

FD = *Die Frage nach dem Ding* (Tübingen: Max Niemeyer Verlag, 1962)

FT = "Die Frage nach der Technik," in *Vorträge und Aufsätze* (Pfullingen: Neske, 1959), pp. 13ff.

GP = *Grundprobleme der Phänomenologie* (Frankfurt am Main: Vittorio Klostermann, 1975)

K = *Kant und das Problem der Metaphysik* (Frankfurt am Main: Vittorio Klostermann, 1951)

N = *Nietzsche.* Zweiter Band (Pfullingen: Neske, 1989)

PG = *Prolegomena zur Geschichte des Zeitbegriffs* (Frankfurt am Main: Vittorio Klostermann, 1979)

SZ = *Sein und Zeit* (Tübingen: Max Niemeyer Verlag, 1957)

UK = "Der Ursprung des Kunstwerks," in *Holzwege* (Frankfurt am Main: Vittorio Klostermann, 1957), pp. 7ff.

UM = "Überwindung der Metaphysik," in *Vorträge und Aufsätze*, pp. 71ff.

WM = *Was ist Metaphysik?* (Frankfurt am Main: Vittorio Klostermann, 1955)

Z = "Seminar in Zähringen 1973," in *Vier Seminare* (Frankfurt am Main: Vittorio Klostermann, 1977), pp. 110ff.

ZW = "Die Zeit des Weltbildes," in *Holzwege*, pp. 69ff.

The Paradox
of Subjectivity

Introduction

Reviving the Question of Subjectivity

My title is taken from Edmund Husserl's last work, *The Crisis of European Sciences*. Paragraph 53 of that posthumous and fragmentary text bears the heading: "The paradox of human subjectivity: being a subject for the world and at the same time being an object in the world"(CR 178). This phrase expresses perfectly the topic to which the following study is devoted.

Debates about the self and the nature of subjectivity have been at the center of modern Western philosophy since Descartes. Recent "Continental" philosophy, whose major figures are still primarily Europeans but which by now includes many English-speakers as well, has brought about a decisive turn in these debates. In an effort to get beyond the preoccupations of modernity altogether and inaugurate a "post-modern" philosophical age, these philosophers have mounted a forceful attack on the concept of the subject or, more broadly, on what is characterized as the "metaphysics of the subject." Though this attack is usually associated with French post-structuralism, and thus with names like Foucault and Derrida, it is also joined by contemporary critical theorists descended from the Frankfurt School of Horkheimer, Adorno, and Marcuse. While the best known of these, Jürgen Habermas, disagrees with dominant French views on rationality, humanism, and even modernity itself, he joins the French philosophers in their opposition to what he calls the philosophy of the subject.[1] For Habermas, too, this term seems to function as a synonym for the modern philosophical tradition as a whole. Philosophers who readily condemn broad generalizations as examples of "totalizing" reason, and who exhort us to pay attention to the particular and the local, do not shrink from summing up the whole history of modern philosophy, from Descartes to Sartre, as variations on a single theme: the metaphysics of the subject.

One irony in this development is that Continental philosophy thus joins hands in an important respect with the heirs of positivism in the analytic tradition. Subjectivity has always been an embarrassment to those who would reduce the world to what can be understood by the natural science of the day. From Ryle's philosophical behaviorism of the 1940s to the efforts of today's neurologically oriented materialists, philosophers in this tradition have labored mightily to eliminate subjectivity because it will not conveniently fit into the seamless materialist ontology that they accept in advance and without argument.

A glance at the current literature on this important topic, in both the Continental and the analytic traditions, suggests that subjectivity will not go away. But the attack has had an enormous benefit. On both sides, it has forced those who are not convinced by it to clarify the reasons why they are not convinced. The materialist-reductionist attack has elicited from philosophers like John Searle and Thomas Nagel, who believe subjectivity must be taken seriously, valuable new accounts of what consciousness is.[2] On the Continental side, where the attack has taken a more historical form, it has forced a reassessment of the modern philosophical tradition, which is the focus of the anti-subjectivist arguments.[3]

This is where this study fits in. I object to the broad strokes with which the modern philosophical tradition is reduced to a single theme and even a single metaphysical doctrine. I return to major figures in that tradition in order to show that crucial differences have been glossed over and ignored. I offer a rereading of the modern tradition, very different from that advanced by the standard attack on the so-called metaphysics of the subject, in order to find there an approach to subjectivity that has somehow been lost in the shuffle. Let me now explain in more detail why I think this is important and how I shall go about it.

The metaphysics of the subject is characterized by its detractors as unfolding inevitably and uniformly from Descartes' *cogito* and culminating in the twentieth century in phenomenology and existentialism. Its central concepts are the ego, consciousness, self-consciousness, self-transparency, self-presence, and self-determination.[4] Dominant until well after World War II, at least in France, this metaphysics is thought to have been gradually undermined when philosophers began to take seriously some powerful ideas from outside the philosophical mainstream. From Marx came the idea of false consciousness; from Freud came the notion of the unconscious; and from linguistics and anthropology came the structuralist conception of thought and language. In spite of their diverse and even incompatible origins, these ideas came together to raise legitimate and troubling questions about some of the key assumptions of the philosophical tradition.

By themselves, however, these extra-philosophical imports would not, I think, have been sufficient to bring on the full-scale repudiation of the philosophical mainstream. Impressive efforts were made, especially in France in the 1950s and 60s by Merleau-Ponty and Ricoeur, to take these ideas seriously and find ways to integrate them with the then-dominant phenomenological approach to the philosophy of consciousness. But these two great thinkers are revisionists rather than revolutionaries, and their conciliatory efforts were not appreciated by their compatriots. France invented the revolution; and while it is not true that the French always prefer revolution to reform, their intellectuals usually do. They were all the more inclined in this direction after the fabled events of May 1968, in which many of them were directly involved, failed to produce a revolution in the streets. But for the philosophers another factor, also not conducive to the idea of compromise, played a key role in the discussion. This was the work of the later Heidegger.[5]

It is in some ways surprising that the ideas of the later Heidegger would be thought compatible with Marxism, psychoanalysis, and structuralism. Heidegger speaks only rarely and negatively, though with some grudging respect, of Marx, and he betrays no acquaintance with Freud or structuralism. Unlike these philosophical outsiders, Heidegger is in some ways the ultimate insider, trained as a philosopher and preoccupied in his work with the great figures of the Western philosophical canon. But then Marxism, psychoanalysis, and structuralism are already strange bedfellows; and bizarre coalitions often turn up in the history of ideas. As an element in the critique of subjectivity, Heidegger's work is legitimately regarded as part of a historical convergence of ideas.

But seen in this historical context, Heidegger's later work is not merely one among a number of equally important developments. It is decisive, in my view, and this for several reasons: In some ways Heidegger's attack on the modern concept of the subject is broader and deeper than those mentioned. If Freud, Marx, and structuralism call into question the modern understanding of human beings, Heidegger links this understanding to that of being as such. He claims thus to attack not just the philosophical anthropology of modern philosophy, but also the ontology or metaphysics on which it is allegedly based. Furthermore, Heidegger's account of the connection between philosophy, science, and technology adds a dimension that is totally lacking in Freud and structuralism, and is much more sophisticated, in the eyes of many, than the one found in Marx. For the French, of course, Marx had in any case long since lost his appeal as a philosopher, even before the worldwide collapse of Marxism as a political force.

But Heidegger's attack on the philosophy of the subject has a further dimension that greatly enhances its appeal and its force: its historical dimension. For philosophers in the Continental tradition, who are accustomed to thinking historically, Heidegger produced a brilliant and detailed portrayal of the origins and development of what they were finding reason elsewhere to question. Actually, the relation between the role of Heidegger and the reception of Marx, Freud, and structuralism in contemporary philosophy should probably be put the other way around: Heidegger's account of the history of modern philosophy prepared a fertile soil for questions planted in the minds of some philosophers by other sources. It provides the broad historical framework in which other critical considerations can find a place. It is Heidegger who provides an account of just what the metaphysics of the subject is and how the philosophers of the modern period, from Descartes to Husserl, fit into it. This account is so widely influential among Continental philosophers today that it is largely taken for granted without question.

Thus the later Heidegger, it seems to me, is the primary figure behind the current rejection of the concept of subjectivity in the Continental tradition. And his historical account of modern philosophy is the key to his influence. It is this historical account that I regard as questionable and worthy of critical review. This is why I begin my study with a chapter on Heidegger's reading of modern philosophy.

It will be clear from what follows that I do not object to the fact that the Heideggerian account is historical or that because of him the attacks on the philosophy of the subject are usually presented in historical form. Indeed, my own response to that account is itself historical. Some critics of Continental philosophy wonder why it is always so preoccupied with the interpretation and reinterpretation of past figures. Why not just talk about subjectivity or the self, rather than deal at such length with what others have said about it? But there are good reasons for this. All theoretical inquiry, including that of the hardest of sciences, is intrinsically historical. Advances do not come out of the blue, but emerge from a theoretical tradition and are directed against prevailing views. But the historical character of inquiry is usually implicit and not always recognized by those involved. Nor should it be, in the case of most disciplines, since the point is to develop theories, not to reflect on how they came about.

Philosophical inquiry is no less, but also probably intrinsically no more, historical than any other. But philosophy, unlike other disciplines, is under the obligation to reflect on its own nature as well as that of its subject matter, to try to understand its own procedures even as it practices them. To philosophize about the self, or about consciousness—or about being, or virtue, or universals—is not to take up some question or problem or puzzle that simply hangs there in the air waiting to be solved, but to enter into a theoretical context that has a history, to approach a topic about which a great deal has been said. Without this historical background the question or problem would not exist, and, more important, it would not be formulated in the way it is. Other disciplines may ignore this fact; philosophy must recognize it if it is to understand fully what it is doing. That most philosophers have indeed recognized this perhaps explains why there has always been a closer connection between philosophy and its history than is the case in physics, say, or psychology.

Some philosophers, of course, including some of the most important, have reacted with irritation to this burden of history and have tried to divest themselves of it, attempting to wipe the slate clean and return to a childlike innocence. Both Descartes and Husserl were of this sort, though the latter changed his views on this subject in his later years. The positivists and their heirs in the analytic tradition share this disdain for history, thinking that one can make a neat division of labor between "doing" philosophy and doing its history. But the results show the naivete of this view. It is not so much the fact that so many wheels have been reinvented, that old ideas are repeatedly put forward as if they were new, which demonstrates the misguidedness of ignoring history. It is rather the constant presence of the philosophical tradition, easily recognizable to anyone familiar with it, hovering in the background of investigations conducted in a supposedly ahistorical manner. Sometimes this presence is explicit even as its significance is not acknowledged. Nothing attests to the historical importance of Descartes so much as the regularity with which he is still attacked and refuted, more than three hundred years after he wrote. A philosopher who must be refuted so many times must have gotten something profoundly right.

As Alasdair MacIntyre has remarked (though not about Descartes): "Genuinely refutable doctrines have to be refuted only once."[6] Though Descartes usually appears in some cartoon version, like Ryle's "ghost in the machine" or Dennett's "Cartesian theater," he is absolutely indispensable to the articulation of theories like theirs.[7]

It is one of the merits of the Continental tradition in philosophy that the historicity of human thought has not only been made a theme but has also been acknowledged as a principle of its own inquiries. Ideas are usually presented in the explicit context of the historical background to which they belong. As part of their theorizing, philosophers devote their attention to the development of the ideas that form the background of what they have to say. But this approach also lends itself to excesses. At one extreme, philosophy can dissolve into philological pedantry. At the other, the past can be made to say what one wants it to say, either in search of support for some view or to provide a foil for attack. This is one way of criticizing Heidegger's reading of modern philosophy, in my view: not that it is historical, but that it is not historical enough.

Yet I do not want to give the impression that I am simply accusing Heidegger of constructing a straw man or of creating historical inaccuracies. Heidegger never writes merely as a historian of philosophy; his account is openly and admittedly a strong interpretation. He is philosophizing, not merely reporting, on the development of modern thought. His interpretation could never have been so influential if it had not been based on a careful, plausible, and profoundly original reading of the philosophers he deals with. But this reading derives some of its strength and plausibility from its sweeping and simplifying character. It is this that I want to challenge. While I think that Heidegger often misconstrues or overlooks certain things that philosophers explicitly say, it is really the broad outlines of his account that I shall try to counter.

In particular, I want to claim that Heidegger ignores the most important division in the modern period, that between the metaphysical and the transcendental traditions. What I am calling the transcendental tradition is inaugurated by Kant and continued in the twentieth century by Husserl. Whereas Heidegger tries to assimilate the work of these philosophers to the metaphysics of modernity, I argue that their work must be understood, as they understood it themselves, as a radical critique of such metaphysics.

My point in this book, of course, is not to criticize Heidegger but to press for this new reading of modern philosophy, and of the place within it of the transcendental tradition. After presenting Heidegger's simplified version of modernity, paying special attention to his reading of Kant and Husserl (chapter 1), I turn my attention to these two philosophers in turn (chapters 2 and 3). I try to show that their theories of the subject, and more broadly their views of the relation between metaphysics and their philosophical projects, are very different from Heidegger's portrayal and much more complex than he thinks. In particular, I concentrate in each case on the paradox referred to in the passage quoted from Husserl at the beginning of this introduction, and articulated by both philosophers as the distinction between transcendental and empirical subjectivity. In my view this distinction, ignored by the later Heidegger, is at the heart of transcendental philosophy. Each philosopher outlines not so much a single theory of the subject, much less a metaphysics of the subject, as two alternate views of the subject that correspond to different ways of conceiving and experiencing the relation between self and world.

In chapter 4 I attempt to bring together the views of Kant and Husserl so as to make clear what I think constitutes the transcendental tradition. I realize that I am using this term in a somewhat unusual way and that my interpretation of it differs in some respects from many standard conceptions—and not just from Heidegger's. I speak of a tradition because I do not think of it as a set of doctrines that would qualify it as a school or even a movement. Most important, it is not the expression of a metaphysics. The transcendental tradition as I conceive it consists instead in a shared conception of the philosophical project as an ongoing critique of human experience and knowledge—including metaphysics. And the transcendental tradition has worked out methods or procedures of reflection for carrying on such a critique. On my interpretation the practice of transcendental philosophy results in the recognition that the two views of the subject, transcendental and empirical, can be neither avoided nor reconciled. Thus, in my view it concludes in paradox.

Most philosophers have not been, and will not be, comfortable with such a paradoxical conclusion. They would seek to eliminate one of the two incompatible views of the self or try to combine them into some grand synthesis. Even Kant and Husserl themselves, it could be argued, were not happy with the paradox, and some of the things they say reflect their desire to overcome it. But they were honest enough to recognize, I think, that their own precepts did not justify or authorize such a move, satisfying as it might be. It is for this reason that they are, for me, the primary figures of the transcendental tradition.

In trying to sum up the transcendental view of the self in chapter 4, however, I have not limited myself to them alone. I have also drawn on the work of other, post-Husserlian thinkers who would not have thought of themselves as part of the transcendental tradition. These include Sartre, Wittgenstein, Nagel, and even the early Heidegger. One could argue, though I do not do so here, that Heidegger was one of those thinkers who became aware of the paradox of subjectivity but could not abide it, finally abandoning the instabilities of the transcendental conception for the consolation of a unifying and more satisfying vision. I would say something similar of another philosopher whom I leave out of the transcendental tradition, even though many would count him in: Fichte. Though I draw some insights from him along the way, I do not treat him as a primary figure in the transcendental tradition. I devote some effort in chapter 4 to distinguishing between transcendental and metaphysical idealism. My claim is that the former is not a metaphysical doctrine at all. But Fichte is the philosopher who begins the conversion of the former into the latter and thus ushers in German Idealism.

To many readers, even those not already persuaded by Heidegger's influential view, my account of modern philosophy and my conception of the transcendental tradition may seem as problematic as Heidegger's does to me. But I have already said that the primary issue is not a narrow conception of historical accuracy. Instead it is a question of plausible interpretation. Heidegger's reading is openly put forward as a strong interpretation, and I am countering it with one of my own. The works of the great philosophers under discussion will probably sustain both. My principal objection to Heidegger's view is not that it is historically incorrect but that it has obscured and consigned to oblivion a view of subjectivity that I think important and worthy of consideration. The ultimate aim of the following pages is not to make a merely historical point but to bring back into view the transcendental conception of the paradox of subjectivity.

ONE

Heidegger on Modern Philosophy and the Transcendental Subject

Like many European thinkers, Heidegger presents his thought in such a way that it is thoroughly intertwined with an account of the tradition out of which it develops. Indeed, it can be argued that after the 1927 publication of his major work, *Being and Time,* this tradition is the central object of his attentions. This may initially seem consistent with the original project of that incomplete work. Its projected, but unpublished, second part was to be devoted to a "destruction of the history of ontology," aimed at the work of Kant, Descartes, and Aristotle (in that order) (SZ 39f).[1] Since a large part of Heidegger's later work deals with the history of philosophy, it could be seen simply as completing the original project in installments, with Plato, Leibniz, Hegel, and Nietzsche thrown in to fill out the picture.

But Heidegger's later focus on the history of philosophy is not entirely consistent with this interpretation. In *Being and Time* his description of the project of "destruction" suggests that, important as it is, it is still secondary or ancillary, that the history of ontology must be destroyed so that the question of being may be addressed afresh. This is one of the many ways in which this work is very traditional: it still seems possible to distinguish between "doing" ontology (as in the completed portion of *Being and Time*) and critically discussing its history. But this distinction practically vanishes in the later work. Here it appears that the only way to address the question of being is to examine the ways in which being has been thought in the tradition. If there is a "task of thinking" that lies beyond the tradition, we cannot yet clearly discern what it is (see EP 66). The best we can do is rethink our tradition, seeking between the lines the unthought possibilities that may point to another beginning. In his latest work the question of being, which Heidegger originally wanted to pose in his own terms, seems indefinitely deferred. For us now, it seems, the primary way to think about being is to think about the ways being has been thought by others.

Thus Heidegger's later work, whether devoted expressly to the work of other philosophers or to such topics as art, language, or technology, generally takes the form of a historical account. Part of the great influence of Heidegger consists in the widespread acceptance of the notion that philosophy can only be done historically. Naturally enough, this has brought with it a broad acceptance of Heidegger's own reading of the history of Western philosophy.

In what follows I shall limit myself to Heidegger's reading of modern philosophy. I shall begin with a discussion of some of the most general and striking features of Heidegger's reading, reflecting on what kind of historical account it is and why it has been so influential. Then I shall turn to the broad outlines of this account as it extends from Descartes through Nietzsche. Finally, I shall turn in detail to Heidegger's treatment of Kant and Husserl, the main representatives of what I am calling the transcendental tradition. This will set the stage for my own readings of these two philosophers in the subsequent chapters.

Heidegger's History of Philosophy

Heidegger's treatment of modern philosophy consists both of studies of individual philosophers and of an account of the whole development from Descartes through Nietzsche and finally Husserl. The reasons for its wide influence are easy to see. Like all of Heidegger's thought it is bold and brilliant. But it has certain features that make it especially appealing to twentieth century academic philosophers whose education consists largely in a certain standard reading of their modern predecessors. Before entering into a more detailed account of Heidegger's history, I want to talk briefly about some of these general features.

First, it manages to be both familiar and new. On the whole it restricts itself to the "canon" of those philosophers and those works that are considered great and that everybody has read. But it gives them a bold new reading with a unified theme: all philosophy is the interpretation of the being of beings.

Second, this unified theme makes possible a new idea of historical development: what is standardly presented as a dialectical movement of conflicting ideas, proceeding by argument and counterargument, is seen instead as a development of variations on a theme. The underlying unity is more important to this reading than the diversity, which is held to be merely superficial.

Third, as for the variations that do take place, the stages that make up the history: these are, of course, generally identified with the major philosophers of the period, beginning with Descartes. But while Heidegger gives us an account of these philosophers' ideas and tells us what is new or distinctive about them, he never tries to tell us *why* they were put forward. That is, he never suggests that Descartes, for example (as he is portrayed in the standard historical account) might have been confronted with certain problems, such as the discrepancy between traditional religion and the new science, and might have come up with his theories as a solution or response to these problems. In other words, a philosopher's ideas are not portrayed as the result of an activity of thinking or reasoning, a human activity that the historian attempts to explain or understand by giving the circumstances, motives, or reasons of the agent. Thus one of the standard features of historical *narrative*—attending to and accounting for human actions—that has traditionally applied to the history of ideas as much as to the history of other human activities is completely missing from Heidegger's account. In *Die Frage nach dem Ding* Heidegger invokes what he calls the "usual picture" of Descartes—confronting the theology of his day, beginning to doubt, and so on, and calls it *ein schlechter Roman*—"at best a bad novel, but not a history in which the movement of being becomes visible" [wenn es hoch kommt, ein schlechter Roman—nur keine Geschichte, in der die Bewegung des Seins sichtbar wird] (FD 77).

It should be noted here that the tendency to look away from human action—and thought as a species of action—as the way of accounting for what happens in history has become extremely widespread. Among philosophers dealing with the history of thought, such as Foucault, Derrida, and Rorty, this tendency can be traced directly to Heidegger. But among historians a similar development seems to have occurred independently. In the 1930s the *Annales* school in France inaugurated a

rapidly spreading trend toward social and economic history that deliberately devalued and ignored the actions of "kings, generals, and bish-
ops" so dear to traditional historiography. These are characterized as
surface ripples on a deeper-lying and slowly changing current of change
hidden from the view of conscious agents.[2] Subjectivity, these historians
hold, rather that explaining anything, is what needs to be explained.

It is obvious that this view of history is perfectly in keeping with
Heidegger's attack on the central role of the subject in modern philosophy, about which I shall be saying more in the course of this chapter.
Modern philosophy glorifies the human subject, Heidegger believes,
and one corollary of this subjectivism would be that historical events
can be traced to the activity of the subject. For Heidegger it is not the
activity of the philosophers that explains the history of philosophy; it
is rather the other way around. Furthermore, the philosophers do not
always understand what is really happening in their own thought.

Fourth, the prime example of this, and of the sense in which Heidegger's account claims to penetrate from the surface to the depths,
concerns the relation of epistemology to ontology. While many of the
classical modern thinkers deal with the problem of knowledge, and
while their thought is typically presented as a progression of epistemological theories, Heidegger constantly asserts that what they are "really" doing is ontology:

> "Theory of knowledge," and what goes by that name, is in essence
> metaphysics and ontology founded on truth conceived as the certainty
> of the securing representation.

> [Die 'Erkenntnistheorie' und was man dafür hält, ist im Grunde die auf
> der Wahrheit als der Gewißheit des sichernden Vorstellens gegründete
> Metaphysik und Ontologie]. (UM 75)[3]

More often than not this claim is made with reference not to what they
say but to the alleged tacit presuppositions of their thought. This move
to the unspoken depths is of course typical of Heidegger's method of
interpretation.

Finally, Heidegger's emphasis on the single underlying theme of
modern philosophy permits a new conception of how the whole of
modern philosophy relates to medieval and especially ancient philosophy, and again this relation is one of unity and continuity rather than
diversity. The focus on knowledge, together with skepticism toward the
possibility of metaphysics, is standardly regarded as that which differentiates the modern from earlier periods in philosophy, which consti-

tutes what is new about it. Heidegger claims that, far from having a different theme and different preoccupations from earlier philosophy, modern philosophy really has the same theme: being.

Thus Heidegger's reading of the history of philosophy is designed to appeal to academically trained philosophers, especially those with a taste for unity over diversity (not unusual among philosophers or, indeed, scholars or scientists generally), those who like to have everything reduced to a single theme. Other branches of philosophy, such as political theory or ethics or logic, which might be thought capable of some independence or at least to have their own history, are passed over in silence or absorbed into ontology.

In spite of all this unity and the tendency to see variations upon a theme, there really is development and change in philosophy, according to Heidegger's story. Furthermore, we must not forget that his reading, unlike the standard notion of *philosophia perennis,* is thoroughly critical and largely negative, though he often denies it. Thus it appeals to academic philosophers, but not complacent ones.

There is a further theme in Heidegger's history that breaks the bonds of the narrowly philosophical and links his story to a much wider sphere. This is the relation of philosophy to modern science and that in turn to all-pervasive technology. This theme, of course, partly accounts for Heidegger's influence outside of academic philosophy and ties him to broader concerns of cultural criticism. Still, academic philosophical temperaments can find much here to please them: again the great diversity of the modern world, including its apparently most non-philosophical aspects, is reduced to an underlying unity, which is again none other than philosophy.[4] So philosophers can still flatter themselves that they are at the center of things, even if they are being told by Heidegger that philosophy is coming or should come to an end and should be replaced by something else.

From *Subiectum* to Subject

After these general characterizations, let us turn to some of the details. It is clear that, for Heidegger, the decisive event that inaugurates modern philosophy is the emergence of the concept of the *subject*. His account of this emergence is focused, unsurprisingly, on Descartes's *cogito*. His claim is that an ontological concept that is already central to ancient and medieval philosophy gets applied to a particular being, the human "I," in a special way.

The ontological concept in question is that of *subiectum*, which is related to *substantia* and is ultimately derived from the Greek *hypokeimenon*, which Heidegger often translates into German as *das Zugrundeliegende*, the underlying support (see UK 12). The concept is ontological in the sense that its primary role since Aristotle is to interpret what it means to be: to be is in the primary sense to be a substance. What substance underlies or supports are its properties or predicates, which thus have being in a dependent or secondary sense.

Understandably enough, Heidegger devotes much critical attention to this concept throughout his career, since it is the key to Western metaphysics or ontology, the chief result of philosophy's attempt to come to terms with the being of beings. It is closely linked to the German term *Ding*, and one of the things that interests him is the connection between the Greek, Latin, and German versions of this notion. In *The Origin of the Work of Art* he asserts that the "groundlessness of Western thought" [Die Bodenlosigkeit des abendländischen Denkens] begins when the Latin version supplants the Greek. In the same place he notes the close connection between the grammatical subject-predicate structure and the metaphysical substance-accident relation, between *Satzbau* and *Dingbau* (UK 13).

From the beginning, of course, Heidegger's stance toward the ontological role of this central concept is deeply critical. In *Being and Time* it is linked with *Vorhandenheit* (presentness at hand) and contrasted with Zuhandenheit (readiness to hand), and there and later in *The Origin of the Work of Art* the claim is made that its dominance has blinded Western philosophy to the importance of *Zeug* (equipment or gear)and *Werk* as modes of being. Most important and most portentous, however, is its application to the human being at the beginning of the modern period. With the turn to the human subject, Heidegger says in the *Grundprobleme der Phänomenologie*, one would have expected that "ontology takes the subject as exemplary entity and interprets the concept of being with a view to the mode of being of the subject, that the *way of being* of the subject becomes an ontological problem. Yet precisely this is not the case" (GP 174). Instead, the old ontological concept is simply transferred without question to the human subject.

The point is made early in *Being and Time*. Heidegger makes the connection there between *hypokeimenon* and *Seelensubstanz* and speaks of the *Verdinglichung des Bewußtseins* (SZ 46). He notes that Dilthey, Scheler, and Husserl attempt to overcome such notions by appealing to alternative concepts like *Leben* and *Person* (SZ 47), but maintains that they don't go far enough—especially Husserl, presumably, since any use of the concept of "subject," he says, is committed ontologically to the *hypokeimenon* whether it realizes it or not (SZ 46).

In *Being and Time*, of course, the point of these criticisms is to introduce and justify the notion of *Dasein* as a replacement for all previous conceptions of human existence. All attempts at philosophical anthropology have suffered under the weight of traditional ontology, treating the human being simply as one *sort* of being among others, one kind of substance or *hypokeimenon*. The question has then been: what essential properties distinguish this being from others? Having reason or language? Having been separately created by God? And so on (see SZ 45ff). The concept of *Dasein* is supposed to avoid this tradition and propose a different approach altogether to human existence.

However, when we turn to Heidegger's account in later works of the beginnings of modern philosophy, larger issues emerge. While certain of these themes from *Being and Time* are carried forward, Heidegger's purpose is no longer merely to portray and criticize a certain ontological conception of human existence. At issue is the role of this conception within the whole of metaphysics, the relation between human being and beings generally.

In *Die Frage nach dem Ding*, after introducing again the connection between the terms *subiectum* and the Greek *hypokeimenon*, Heidegger describes what he calls the "groundshaking transformation" [grundstürzender Wandel] that occurs in Descartes' philosophy:

> Prior to Descartes every thing that was present at hand for itself counted as a "subject"; but now the "I" becomes the privileged subject, that in relation to which the other things are determined as such.

> [Bis zu Descartes galt als 'Subjekt' jedes für sich vorhandene Ding; jetzt aber wird das 'Ich' zum ausgezeichneten Subjekt, zu demjenigen, mit Bezug auf welches die übrigen Dinge erst als solche sich bestimmen.]
> (FD 81f)

The point here is thus not merely the central role of the notion of *hypokeimenon* or *subiectum*, nor is it the fact that this concept is used to interpret human existence ontologically. The point is that the human *Ich* becomes the *privileged hypokeimenon* and that all other things acquire a mode of being that is determined by reference to this privileged being. They are things, but they get their very *Dingheit* from their relation to the subject. They are "essentially such that they stand as other in relation to the 'subject', lying over against it as *obiectum* [wesenhaft solches, was als ein anderes in Beziehung zum 'Subjekt' steht, ihm entgegenliegt als obiectum"]. They become "objects" (FD 82).

In *Die Frage nach dem Ding* Heidegger has a comment on the word *object* that introduces a certain irony into his account. According to him, prior to Descartes the term *obiectum* meant something given "im bloßen Sichvorstellen," that is, something merely imagined like a golden mountain. (This is, in fact, how the term "objective reality" is still used by Descartes.) Thus it referred to something that in the modern sense is precisely not objective but merely subjective. Heidegger claims that the meanings of *obiectum* and *subiectum* have thus been reversed: where previously the "subject" (i.e., substance) was the real and the "objective" merely imaginary, now it is the "objective" that is real and the subjective that is not.

Heidegger attaches great significance to this meaning reversal. It is this that he calls a "grundstürzender Wandel des Daseins, d.h. der Lichtung des Seins des Seienden," an earthshaking event in *genuine* or *authentic* history—that is, the history of the "Offenbarkeit des Seins"—which is necessarily hidden from the normal eye [dem gewöhnlichen Auge notwendig verborgen] (FD 82).

This may strike the reader as a loud fanfare for what seems only a mildly interesting observation, and one that may not even be that original. Heidegger uses such strong language here, it seems to me, because the irony of this reversal is a *double* one. Beneath the surface of a language that metaphysically valorizes the "objective" over the "subjective," Heidegger wants ultimately to say, lies an ontology that does precisely the reverse. For in spite of all orientation toward the objective, in modern philosophy and especially science, it is the subject, now conceived as the "Ich," which exists in the primary sense, while the objective is in the end reduced to something secondary. The ultimate irony is thus that beneath the surface, the older ontological "weights" attached to *obiectum* and *subiectum*, rather than being reversed, are actually preserved.

Heidegger's account of modern philosophy is really the story of how this happens (n.b.: not why but how). As noted, in the Cartesian philosophy things become essentially "what stands as an other in relation to the 'subject', lying over against it" [was als ein anderes in Beziehung zum 'Subjekt' steht, ihm entgegenliegt]. They are other than the subject and stand over against the subject—*ihm gegenüberstehen*—thus becoming *Gegen-stände*. (UM 74). There is a fundamental otherness to the object that is never really lost—it is not merely a figment of the imagination (N 169). Yet that very otherness is determined by reference to the subject, and the task of modern thought, according to Heidegger, is to overcome that otherness and reduce it to the same.

The relation of subject to object is initially conceived as a knowing relation, but the "problem" of knowledge can arise because subject and object have been ontologically determined as knower and known. It is in this sense that ontology or metaphysics is always prior to epistemology. Interpreting the being of beings as subject and object reflects a certain "basic stance toward being" [Grundstellung zum Sein] taken by "historical Dasein" [das geschichtliche Dasein] in the modern age (FD 74). Every age (*Zeitalter*) has its own "*metaphysische Grundstellung*" (ZW 96), but Heidegger never explains why a new one should arise to replace the old. It is in this sense that the "why" is missing in his account.

The modern conception of beings as objects of knowledge brings with it a specific conception of what knowing is. Descartes' "ego cogito" becomes the *first principle*, or *Grundsatz*, of a mathematically conceived reason based on the principle of non-contradiction (*Widerspruchsatz*) and the principle of sufficient reason (*Satz vom Grund*). Reason, or Logos, now conceived in mathematical terms, resides in or emanates from the subject rather than belonging to the nature of things generally (FD 84f). It takes the form of a method or procedure (*Forschung* is *Vorgehen* [ZW 71]) carried out by the subject. Descartes' quest for certainty is interpreted by Heidegger as a quest to secure (*sicherstellen*) the object. The "standing" of the *Gegen-stand* may seem to signify a certain permanence and independence (*Ständigkeit des Bestandes* [UM 74]) But "What stands is in its standing essentially related to the positing of representation as the securing of having before oneself" [Der Bestand in seinem Stand ist wesenhaft bezogen auf das Stellen des Vor-stellens als des sichernden Vor-sich-habens] (UM 74).

In every representation, where "*ich stelle vor*," the "I" is also represented. Descartes' *cogito* is really "*cogito me cogitare*": human consciousness is essentially self-consciousness (N 155). To represent something is to represent it *to* oneself, thus "the person who represents also represents himself in each act of representing—not after the fact but in advance" [stellt sich der vorstellende Mensch in jedem Vorstellen mit ein—nicht nachträglich sondern zum voraus] (N 154). In the Nietzsche lectures Heidegger brings a fairly standard commentary on the importance and the nature of self-consciousness in modern philosophy, but in the context of his own reading of metaphysics it has a special significance. The "I" becomes the subject of all representations, but it is also the prime and ever-present object; it too exists only insofar as it is present (*anwesend* or *vorhanden*) to a subject.

Representation and the Will to Power

In using the language of *Vorstellung* Heidegger is already forging the link between modern metaphysics, science, and technology. The term *Vorstellung* is central to Kant's first Critique, but is used there in a way that makes it more or less equivalent to the Latin, French, and English term *idea* (*idée*) used by his modern predecessors. Perhaps on this basis, Heidegger permits himself to read the German term back into Descartes: "If we understand *cogitare* as *vor-stellen* in this literal sense, we come closer to the Cartesian concept of *cogitatio* and *perceptio*." [Wenn wir cogitare als vor-stellen in diesem wörtlichen Sinn verstehen, dann kommen wir dem Descartesschen Begriff der cogitatio und perceptio schon näher] (N 151). The German version allows Heidegger the advantage of the connection with *Stellen* (setting, placing, setting up, ordering) and later with *Gestell* (framework) that is central to his treatment of technology. *Percipere* in the sense of Vorstellen means to take possession of something (*in Besitz nehmen*), to master something (*einer Sache sich bemächtigen*), to set it up before oneself (N 151).

The purpose of knowledge in the modern sense is to make beings "*dem Vorstellen verfügbar*," to render them available to representation (ZW 80). To avail oneself of them is to be able to explain retrospectively (*nachrechnen*) or predict (*vorausberechnen*). Thus to represent is to calculate. "Only what becomes an object in this sense *is*, counts as being" [Nur was dergestalt Gegenstand wird, *ist*, gilt als seiend]. Truth becomes the certainty of representation (ZW 80).

> Representing is no longer taking in what is present . . . , no longer self-unconcealing for . . . , but rather taking hold of and grasping . . . It is not that what is present holds sway; rather, assault rules.

> [Vorstellen ist nicht mehr Vernehmen des Anwesenden . . . nicht mehr das Sich-entbergen für . . . , sondern das Ergreifen und Begreifen von . . . Nicht das Anwesende waltet, sondern der Angriff herrscht.] (ZW 100).

Knowledge is thus conceived as an active intervention in the world, an overcoming of being (*Bewältigung des Seienden*) (ZW 84), a grasping and determining of the object by rendering it objective, reducing it to representation. The world becomes a world-picture.

This active character of knowing is best seen when Heidegger turns his attentions from Descartes to Leibniz. This philosopher makes the explicit connection between *percipere* and *appetitio,* which Heidegger translates as *Anstrebung* or striving. This is in turn interpreted by Leibniz as force (*vis*) or energy. Here begins the attempt to bring together representation and will or desire that culminates in Schopenhauer and Nietzsche. Just as reason emanates from the subject and applies itself through procedure or method to things, so desire or force emanates from the subject as well, and in the end they come to the same thing.

This point is extremely important for Heidegger's story of modern philosophy, as he indicates in the following passage:

> For the modern history of metaphysics the term subjectivity expresses the full essence of being only if we think not merely, and not even primarily, of the representational character of being, but when *appetitus* and its unfolding as the basic character of being have become evident. Being is, since the full beginning of modern metaphysics, *will.*

> [Für die neuzeitliche Geschichte der Metaphysik spricht aber der Name Subjektivität nur dann das volle Wesen des Seins aus, wenn nicht nur und nicht einmal vorwiegend an den Vostellungscharakter des Seins gedacht wird, sondern wenn der appetitus und seine Entfaltung als Grundzug des Seins offenkundig geworden sind. Sein ist seit dem vollen Beginn der neuzeitlichen Metaphysik *Wille.*] (N 452)

Will in this modern sense encompasses "the will of reason or the will of the spirit . . . , the will of love or the will to power" [der Wille der Vernunft oder der Wille des Geistes . . . , der Wille der Liebe oder der Wille zur Macht] (N 452).

In the end, in Leibniz subjectivity becomes the model of being as such: the subject (monad) is not just the privileged being; in the end all being is subject, to be is to be a subject. But this subject is of course not the ancient *hypokeimenon* but the modern, Cartesian subject. For Leibniz, to be is either to be a subject or to be a representation belonging to a subject. For all beings that appear other than subjective, "to be is to be represented by a representing subject" [Seiendheit besagt jetzt Vor-gestelltheit des vor-stellenden Subjekts] (N 169); that is, to be other than a subject is to be an object for a subject, to exist in a way that is essentially dependent on the subject. Reducing the world to a calculable representation is the role of knowledge in general, modern scientific knowledge in particular. But this is really in the end identical with the role of technology. Though modern science begins to develop in the seventeenth century and technology really flourishes only in the late eighteenth, Heidegger can say that modern technology is in essence historically earlier than science (FT 30). Its possibility animated science's conception of being from the start.

For Heidegger this tendency in modern philosophy to make subjectivity the model of being finds its highest expression and best formulation in a much quoted passage from the preface to Hegel's *Phenomenology*: "The true is to be conceived and expressed not as substance but rather as subject" [das Wahre nicht als Substanz, sondern eben so sehr als Subjekt aufzufassen und auszudrücken] (EP 68). In Hegel's dialectic, the subject transcends itself toward the object as other, but only in order ultimately to overcome the otherness of the object and return to itself, bringing the object along with it. The principle of self-consciousness, which is articulated in Descartes, is in Hegel expanded into a lengthier and more powerful itinerary of self-relation. This dialectical conception functions equally well as a description of knowledge and as a characterization of technology's domination and subjugation of nature. Nietzsche's concept of the will to power is an equally good description of both phenomena.

Metaphysics, Method, and Technology

Let me sum up our account so far. For the late Heidegger all philosophy is ontology or metaphysics, whose task is to think about beings as a whole with respect to their being (EP 61). For ancient and medieval philosophy, this thinking finds its expression in the concept of substance as *hypokeimenon, substantia*, or *subiectum*. Substance is the underlying, persisting foundation that supports everything else. To be is either to *be* a substance or to be a property or predicate of a substance. Substance exists in the primary sense; everything else exists "in" substance and thus has a merely secondary and dependent way of existing.

Modern metaphysics is a variation on this theme, with subtle but important differences. Beginning with Descartes, the human or conscious "subject," the cogito, assumes the role of substance or primary existence. As Heidegger puts it in one place, all metaphysics is characterized by "subjectity" [*Subiectität*], but in modern philosophy this is transformed into "subjectivity" (N 450ff). To be is either to *be* such a subject or to exist *in* such a subject, and thus again to have a secondary and derivative mode of being. But to exist "in" a subject is now not so much to be a predicate or property of it, as to be an object or representation for it. In virtue of the principle of self-consciousness the subject even has the status of object or representation for itself.

And primary being or subjectivity, following Leibniz, Hegel, and Nietzsche, is conceived as the activity, striving, or will, which takes over all being by objectifying it and reducing it to calculable representations, framing it within a world-picture that is a product of subjective (human) activity.

This notion of activity is embodied in various notions of method or procedure, from Descartes' *Discours* and *Regulae* through Hegel's dialectical method, and finds its expression as well in such notions as scientific method, research, and experimental and technical procedure. Modern philosophy culminates in the development and success of technology. "The end of philosophy reveals itself as the triumph of the manipulable ordering of a scientific-technical world." [Das Ende der Philosophie zeigt sich als der Triumph der steuerbaren Einrichtung einer wissenschaftlich-technischen Welt . . .] (EP 65).

So far I have made almost no mention of two philosophers who are especially important figures in the development of modern philosophy for Heidegger, namely, Kant and Husserl. Because they are so important for our own project in what follows, I have left them for last. For us it is important to take note of the fact that Heidegger understands these two thinkers as exemplary figures in the development I have just described, from Descartes through modern technology; and it is important to see how this is so.

Heidegger on Kant

As we have seen, Heidegger announces early in *Being and Time* that he will devote a lot of attention to Kant in the second part of the work, and *Kant und das Problem der Metaphysik* appears as an independent work shortly after *Being and Time*, presumably containing what was to have been included in the larger work. But the published part of *Being and Time* already contains many references to Kant and provides a preview of what is to come. In addition, we now have the publication in the *Gesamtausgabe* of Heidegger's lectures from the 1920s, in particular *Die Grundprobleme der Phänomenologie* of 1927, which contains lengthy sections on Kant.[5]

Heidegger's attitude toward Kant in these early texts is both positive and negative. He thinks that Kant was on the brink of discovering the link between *Dasein* and temporality in the first half of the *Critique of Pure Reason*, but that he "shrank back" (SZ 23) from this discovery and reverted to a doctrine much more in line with the modern tradition to which he belonged.

In keeping with his reading of all the modern philosophers Heidegger asserts that Kant's doctrine in the first Critique is really metaphysical rather than epistemological or critical (K 13f, GP 180ff.). Metaphysics is identified with ontology, here as elsewhere, but in these earlier works Heidegger identifies his own project with both. Quoting a passage in which Kant says that his inquiries culminate in the question "Was ist der Mensch?" (K 187), Heidegger is able to read Kant as moving toward an understanding of the being of *Dasein*. But Kant is hindered by the modern interpretation of man primarily as knowing subject.

Heidegger's thesis is that in spite of his attack in the first Critique on the substantivization of the "I," Kant

> slips ... back into the *same* inappropriate ontology of the substantial whose ontic foundations he had theoretically denied for the "I"

> [gleitet ... doch wieder in *dieselbe* unangemessene Ontologie des Substanzialen zurück, deren ontische Fundamente er theoretisch dem Ich abgesprochen hat.] (SZ 319)

Interpreting the I as the transcendental "I think," underlying the activity of combining and relating its representations, Kant ascribes to it essentially the role of *hypokeimenon* (SZ 319). Though he moves, especially in the doctrine of the schematism, toward an understanding of the temporalizing activity of Heidegger's *Dasein*, Kant interprets the "I" as "stehendes und bleibendes," the standing and abiding *res* that underlies all change. In the end Kant's view of the subject is no different from that of Descartes: "the I, the ego, is for him as for Descartes the *res cogitans, res, something [etwas]* that thinks" (GP 177). It is the metaphysical subject whose predicates are *cogitationes, Vorstellungen.* "This subject is not just *different* from its predicates, it *has* them as known, that is, as *objects*" (GP 178). Correctly seeing that the I is not *in* time, like an event, Kant concludes that it is timeless, like an unchanging thing (K 174f).

Thus, in the 1920s Kant is subjected to the same sort of critique Heidegger directs at other modern philosophers. They understand the being of beings in general as substantiality or *Vorhandenheit,* which is bad enough, and go on to make the much more serious mistake of interpreting the being of *Dasein* in the same way. Thus, in spite of the rich possibilities to be found in his work, Kant is in the end but a link in the chain that leads from Descartes to Hegel:

> Because Kant for the first time made explicit what was already prefigured in Descartes and Leibniz, that the I is the true *subjectum*—in Greek

the true substance, *hypokeimenon*—Hegel could then say: the true substance is subject, or the true sense of substantiality is subjectivity.

[Weil bei Kant zum ersten Mal explizit, wenn auch schon bei Descartes und vor allem bei Leibniz vorgebildet, das Ich das eigentliche subjectum ist, griechisch gesprochen die eigentliche Substanz, *hypokeimenon,* kann Hegel dann sagen: Die eigentliche Substanz ist das Subjekt, oder der eigentliche Sinn der Substanzialität ist die Subjektivität.] (GP 178f)

Heidegger's conclusion is that finally Kant contributes to the misunderstanding of human existence that Heidegger seeks to put right with his fundamental ontology.

After *Being and Time* and *Kant and the Problem of Metaphysics,* Heidegger's critical reading of Kant develops parallel to his reading of the other figures of modern philosophy. For one thing, the attempt to find, in Kant's work, positive steps toward a genuine ontology is practically abandoned. Kant is treated along with Descartes and others as a representative of the modern "metaphysics and ontology" that Heidegger studies in order to overcome. In the earlier works Heidegger identifies his own task with ontology and metaphysics; later these terms are used strictly to designate the Western tradition that forms the object of Heidegger's critical attentions.

In a sense, then, we could say that it is only the negative side of Kant that now interests Heidegger; but the negative side has also subtly changed. The issue is no longer merely the misunderstanding of *Dasein,* but rather Kant's participation in the metaphysics of the subject. Again denying any distinction between ontology and epistemology or (in Kantian terms) critique, Heidegger calls "*Transzendentalphilosophie*" simply "*die neuzeitliche Gestalt der Ontologie*"—the modern form of ontology (UM 74). The claim that Kant substantivizes the human being remains part of this, of course, but equally important is the more general notion that "the beingness of entities is thought as presence *for* the securing representation. Beingness is now objectness" [die Seiendheit des Seienden als die Anwesenheit *für* das sicherstellende Vorstellen gedacht wird. Seiendheit ist jetzt Gegenständigkeit] (UM 74f). We have already noted that Heidegger seizes on the term *Vorstellen* in order to express the connection, in modern philosophy as a whole, between representation and technology, and we noted that this is a central Kantian term. Given the importance of language for Heidegger, Kant could be seen to have played a central role in modern metaphysics by this terminological choice alone. The development that begins with Descartes, whereby the essence of reality (*Wirklichkeit*) is seen as the "*Gegenständlichkeit des*

Gegenstandes (Objektivität des Objekts)," is fully grasped in all clarity only by Kant [erst von Kant in aller Klarheit . . . begriffen] (N433). In his notion of the "original synthetic unity of transcendental apperception" (as Heidegger styles it [N 463]), Kant also fully articulates the principle of self-consciousness originally formulated by Descartes.

Equally important is the manner in which Kant goes beyond Leibniz in portraying knowledge as an activity and objects known as something like its products (see FD 142–43). "Representation brings about the ordering of the object's standing over-against" [Das Vorstellen erwirkt die Zustellung des Entgegenstehens des Gegenstandes] (N433). (Heidegger warns us not to interpret this to mean the object is a psychological product.) What is more, Heidegger emphasizes that Kant calls the understanding a faculty of rules (*Vermögen der Regeln*) and even a source of rules (FD 147), which ties in with the modern conception of knowledge as procedure or method. This is a crucial step on the way from Leibniz to Hegel and ultimately to Nietzsche's conception of subjectivity as will to power.

Heidegger on Husserl

Heidegger's relation to Husserl was always, to say the least, complicated. *Being and Time* is, of course, dedicated to Husserl and contains references to him that are almost exclusively positive. The lectures of the 1920s, especially those collected under the title *Prolegomena zur Geschichte des Zeitbegriffs*, document better than *Being and Time* Heidegger's critical stance toward Husserl's conception of phenomenology, but even they are veiled in the kind of deference Heidegger obviously thought he owed to his mentor ("Even today I still regard myself as a learner in relation to Husserl," he writes [PG 168]). In those lectures, Heidegger devotes a lengthy and sympathetic exposition to the development of Husserl's early thought, even defending it against its neo-Kantian critics (PG 41ff.). He regards intentionality as the central "discovery" of phenomenology and gives a Husserlian account of perception (PG 46ff.). He devotes special attention to the notion of categorial intuition in the *Logical Investigations,* a notion that suggests to him that being can be experienced, can become a phenomenon (PG 63ff.).

For Heidegger categorial intuition establishes the essential connection between phenomenology and ontology; but this is a connection Husserl did not appreciate. This point is the focus of Heidegger's critical remarks on Husserl in the lectures. He reproaches Husserl for "neglect of the question of the being of the intentional" (PG 148) and indeed for neglecting "the question of the sense of being itself" (PG 157), and of the being of man. Heidegger's critique of Kant's substantivization of the subject is aimed at Husserl's "transcendental ego" as well. In general, it is clear that he found Husserl's transcendental turn, after the *Logical Investigations*, a diversion from the genuine idea of phenomenology.

When Heidegger turns, in the mid-1930s, to his historical preoccupations, Husserl practically vanishes from his pages along with others who were frequently cited in his earlier works, such as Jaspers, Scheler, Cassirer, and Dilthey. Though Dilthey and Husserl belonged to older generations, Heidegger doubtless regarded all these philosophers as contemporaries from whom he wished to distance himself. Some, of course, had become politically unmentionable (including Husserl); and in any case they were not taken to belong to the history of metaphysics, with which Heidegger was now preoccupied. This history was supposed to have come to an end with Nietzsche.

It is thus all the more interesting that Husserl should turn up again in some of Heidegger's very latest writings. One is the 1964 text "Das Ende der Philosophie und die Aufgabe des Denkens," where he is given a place of honor alongside Hegel as a representative of modern metaphysics. To be sure, this is an honor that Husserl along with the others might not have accepted with a great deal of pleasure, since what they supposedly represent is a mode of thinking that has now come (or is coming) to an end and needs to be replaced. The point here is to ask: "What task is reserved for thinking at the end of philosophy?" [Welche Aufgabe bleibt dem Denken noch vorbehalten am Ende der Philosophie?] (EP66).

It is in this text that Heidegger's complicated attitude toward the history of modern philosophy receives some of its most interesting formulations. He indicates that he is in search of a task for thinking that has been closed off precisely by (Western) philosophy and may be accessible now that philosophy is finished. Here he admits that his reader might come to the (not unreasonable) conclusion that he is portraying philosophy as a *Geschichte des bloßen Verfalls* (a history only of decline) because philosophy has proved to be inadequate to the true task of thinking. He admits that this might be interpreted as "arrogance which places itself above the greatness of the thinkers of philosophy" (EP 66).

Not so, Heidegger assures us; and here his modesty knows no bounds. What he is attempting, he says, actually falls short of the greatness of the philosophers [bleibt... notwendig hinter der Größe der Philosophen zurück]. It depends precisely on them, on "looking back at the whole of the history of philosophy" [den Rückblick in das Ganze der Geschichte der Philosophie]. It needs to think about "the historicity of that which secures for philosophy a possible history" [die Geschichtlichkeit dessen . . . was der Philosophie eine mögliche Geschichte gewährt]. Unlike philosophy, the task Heidegger envisages will have neither a direct nor even an indirect effect on the public life of the technical-scientific-industrial age. In any case its purpose is not to found anything but only to prepare for a possibility "whose outline is obscure and whose coming is uncertain." In the end Heidegger refers only to "*das vermutete Denken,*" "*die vermutete Aufgabe des Denkens,*" a thinking or a task of thinking that is merely surmised or guessed at (EP 66).

It is in this tentative and uncertain context that Husserl now enters the scene, along with Hegel, as a representative of modern philosophy. Heidegger is himself in search of "*die Sache des Denkens*"—the matter or the issue of thinking *after* philosophy, and he turns to these two thinkers for what they said about the "*Sache*" of philosophy. Each of these thinkers called philosophy back "*zur Sache*" or "*zu den Sachen selbst.*" What did they think the "*Sache*" of philosophy was, what did they think philosophy was really *about?*

Though he admits that there are great differences between Hegel and Husserl, Heidegger thinks they both conceive of philosophy in terms of the connection between subjectivity and method. Thus they conform to the familiar and unified picture developed by Heidegger for modern philosophy as a whole. The matter of philosophy is really decided in advance for both philosophers by virtue of their belonging to the modern tradition. The "subjectivity of consciousness" is what both of them are after, and both conceive of their task as that of developing a procedure for bringing subjectivity to demonstrable givenness [zur ausweisbaren Gegebenheit] (EP 69). Heidegger mentions Husserl's "principle of all principles" from *Ideas* 1, which is embodied in the transcendental reduction. Through it Husserl seeks to ground "the objectivity of all objects"—which Heidegger equates with "*das Sein des Seienden*"—in and through subjectivity. Transcendental subjectivity reveals itself (and here Heidegger is able to quote Husserl verbatim) as "the sole absolute entity" [das einzige absolute Seiende] (EP 70).

What is more, Husserl shares with his modern predecessors the preoccupation with *method*. Through the phenomenological *epoche*, after all, any independence the object might have is taken away. The method is described as a *reduction;* it reduces the world to the status of intentional object or representation. In the process transcendental subjectivity achieves full *Gegebenheit* to itself. Though he does not say it, Heidegger might have characterized Husserl's method, as he does that of the other modern philosophers, as a roundabout way of describing the technological subjugation of the world.

Husserl is also the subject of an intense discussion in the Zähringen Seminar of 1973, just three years before Heidegger's death. As in the 1927 lectures, Heidegger begins with a very positive account of Husserl's notion of categorial intuition, a notion that had been helpful to Heidegger in his early thinking about being. Heidegger considers it a great advance, especially over Kant and the neo-Kantians, that categories themselves, and even being, can be said to be given in our experience, rather than functioning as a priori forms. "With these analyses of categorial intuition Husserl freed being from its tie to judgment" [Mit jenen Analysen der kategorialen Anschauung hat Husserl das Sein aus seiner Festlegung auf das Urteil befreit] (Z 377).

However, Husserl did not go the next step and ask what "being" meant [was besagt Sein?], since he took for granted "that 'being' means being-an-object" [daß 'Sein' Gegenstand-Sein bedeutet] (Z 378). And for Husserl, of course, object means object for consciousness. In Heidegger's early work consciousness (Bewußtsein) is replaced by Dasein as the focus. Heidegger devotes some discussion to why this occurred and what the connection is between Dasein and Bewußtsein.

Consciousness, Heidegger says, is linked with immanence. To be conscious of something is to have it *in* my consciousness. Adding the concept of intentionality to consciousness, as Husserl does, changes nothing. "In spite of intentionality, Husserl remains closed up in immanence" [So bleibt Husserl der Intentionalität entgegen doch in der Immanenz eingeschlossen] (Z 382). In *Being and Time*, by contrast, objects or things are not in consciousness but in the world.

It is impossible to break out of the realm of immanence, Heidegger says, as long as one's point of departure is the *ego cogito*, "for the basic constitution of the *ego cogito* is (exactly as it is that of Leibniz's monad) that it has no windows through which anything could come in or go out" [denn es liegt in der Grundverfassung des Ego cogito (wie ebenso in der der Monade bei Leibniz), daß es keinerlei Fenster hat, durch die etwas hereinkommen oder hinausgehen könnte] (Z 383). *Dasein*, by contrast, means already being outside itself, "ek-static"; we encounter things "face-to-face, not by means of a representation" [von Angesicht zu Angesicht und nicht mehr vermittels einer Vorstellung] (Z 384). For example, "When I think in memory of René Char in Les Busclats, who or what is given to me?—René Char himself! Not some sort of 'picture' through which I would be indirectly related to him" [Wenn ich in der

Erinnerung an René Char in Les Busclats denke, wer oder was ist mir
dabei gegeben?—René Char selbst! Nicht Gott weiß welches 'Bild'
durch das ich mittelbar auf ihn bezogen wäre] (Z 384).

Thus Heidegger presents Husserl as conforming perfectly to the
pattern of the tradition, as yet another variation on the theme of modern metaphysics. Like everyone else, whether he realizes it or not Husserl is "really" trying to think the being of beings. In the first instance
to be is to be an object or representation. "Gegebenheit" is just Husserl's version of *Anwesenheit* or *Vorhandenheit*. But this in turn means to
be an object or representation for the subject; and of course the subject
even has this status for itself. The latter is thus being in the primary
sense "das einzige absolute Seiende." Transcendental subjectivity is just
the latest version of the ancient *hypokeimenon*.

Thus Heidegger presents us with an account of the history of modern
philosophy as a unified development—or, as I said before, as a set of
variations on a theme. All philosophy has been the project of thinking
the being of beings. From the earliest times, the being of beings has
been interpreted as subject in the sense of *hypokeimenon* or substance.
The variation on this theme that marks the beginning of the modern
epoch is that subject or substance is now viewed principally as the
human subject conceived as knower; while for everything else, to be is
to be an object or representation for such a subject. Knowledge is
understood as the ordering and mastery of the world. A further variation, then, is that man's knowing relation to being is appetite, desire,
or ultimately the will to power.

As we might expect, and as we have now seen, transcendental philosophy, as conceived by both Kant and Husserl, is in no way an ex-
ception to this development. Just as epistemology is dismissed by
Heidegger as the genuine preoccupation of the early moderns, so transcendental philosophy is seen as just the modern form of metaphysics
or ontology. Indeed, Heidegger seems to make no distinction between
epistemology and transcendental philosophy, except perhaps to interpret the latter as a particular example of the former. This, of course,
is not an uncommon view among philosophers and historians of philosophy. Heidegger goes farther, however, in claiming that what the
epistemologists and transcendental philosophers are "really" doing is
metaphysics or ontology, that is, providing an interpretation of the being of beings.

The metaphysics these philosophers propound, it seems, is, according to Heidegger, nothing other than what has been called idealism—

though this is subject to some unexpected variations. The knowing subject takes the role of substance; everything else is reduced to its properties, whether as immanent in consciousness, object for the subject, or, as in transcendental philosophy, construct and product of subjective activity. All take for granted the modern scientific approach according to which thing and world are what they are only insofar as they can be manipulated, calculated, predicted, and controlled.

There are many features of modern philosophical history to which this interpretation seems to do violence. All those debates about skepticism and the possibility of knowledge, those disputes between the realists and the idealists, seem reduced to meaningless chatter—*Gerede*, perhaps. Present-day scientific realists, no doubt, would not accept what seems to be the claim that there is "really" no difference between their views and those of the idealists.

This bold and controversial interpretation is not as implausible as it seems, and there are arguments to be made in its defense. Where it goes wrong, as I have said, is in its treatment of transcendental philosophy, its failure to recognize what is distinctive about it. It is Heidegger's interpretation of Kant and Husserl that I wish to call into question. As we turn in detail to these philosophers in the chapters that follow I shall be providing support for the claim that transcendental philosophy, contrary to what Heidegger says, is neither epistemology nor metaphysics. It is not a metaphysics of the subject, and the subject, as conceived by these philosophers, is not a metaphysical *hypokeimenon*. Transcendental philosophy, conceived as critique by Kant and as phenomenology by Husserl, attempts to revamp the philosophical project, to pose new questions rather than provide new answers to old questions. In the process it reopens the question of the subject in ways that most interpreters have not appreciated. Though Heidegger is not the only philosopher who has contributed to this misunderstanding, his misreading is perhaps the most egregious and at the same time the most influential. It is for this reason that I have begun with his account of modern philosophy and of the transcendental tradition.

Kant

Subjectivity and Apperception

Is Kant's philosophy a metaphysics of the subject? Certainly not, if we take him at his word in the *Critique of Pure Reason*. That work is indeed *about* metaphysics, but it is not itself a work *of* metaphysics. In fact, its central question is whether metaphysics, as conceived by the philosophical tradition, is even possible as a science; and Kant concludes that it is not. And since traditional metaphysics, according to Kant, addresses itself to the problems of God, freedom, and immortality, (A3B7), [1] and since at least two of these problems involve metaphysical claims about the nature of the self, a metaphysics of the self in this sense seems to be ruled out. And indeed, as we know, important sections of the *Critique* are devoted to showing how metaphysical claims about the immortality and the freedom of the human subject cannot be supported. Far from offering us a metaphysics of the subject, then, Kant seems not merely to exempt himself from such a project, but even to declare it impossible for anyone else.

But this interpretation turns on Kant's very narrow definition of metaphysics. Even he does not rule out the term, provided it is suitably redefined, and he endorses the project of a metaphysics of nature (Axxi) and later a metaphysics of morals.[2] And if others attribute to him a metaphysics of the subject, it might seem that there are good reasons for doing so. For one thing, he has a great deal to say *about* the subject, and what he does say seems to conform to at least part of what Kant himself considers metaphysics to be. It may not consist of claims about freedom and immortality, but it is, like such claims, a priori, that is, independent of experience. Perhaps more important, the subject is after all not merely one topic among others in Kant's major work. The celebrated "Copernican turn," his great innovation, has it that "objects must conform to our knowledge" (Bxvii) rather than the other way around—that is, our understanding determines a priori what is to count as objects and how they may be related. Kant goes so far as to say that human understanding has the function of "prescribing laws to nature, and even of making nature possible" (B159f.) Since the understanding in turn is conceived by Kant as the spontaneous synthetic activity of the subject, it is no wonder that Kant is taken by some of his successors to be the initiator of a radical form of idealism, a theory that can be called "metaphysical," if not in Kant's own sense then in most traditionally accepted senses of the term, and that is centered on the subject in a way that surpasses all previous idealisms. Furthermore, in the moral philosophy the self is distinguished by its autonomy, its prescribing laws to itself. A self that legislates both to itself and to nature is a sovereign self in an almost blasphemously extreme sense, seemingly subjected to no power, natural or moral, beyond itself. If this is not a metaphysics of the subject, it might be asked, what is?

But this picture of Kant's thought is painted in very broad strokes and ignores the context from which his views emerge and the manner in which they are put forward. If we are to understand these we must look in more detail at the "theory of the subject" as it is found in the *Critique of Pure Reason* in light of the general problem to which that work addresses itself.

Transcendental and Empirical Self-Consciousness

Any understanding of what Kant has to say about the subject must begin at that place in the *Critique* where his views on this topic are most explicitly put forward, namely, in the second edition version of the Transcendental Deduction. What is generally noticed there is the emergence of the notion of a "transcendental" subject and its companion concept, the empirical subject. But the status of these notions, and of the distinction between them, is as much in dispute as are other aspects of this notoriously difficult section of the *Critique*. Everyone seems to agree that the Transcendental Deduction is the heart of Kant's doctrine; in light of this it is all the more significant that there is little agreement on what it accomplishes, or even on what it is meant to accomplish, what its structure is, what—if any—arguments it contains, and so on.[3]

I want to focus our attention here on Kant's views on the subject. It would be desirable if we could restrict ourselves to that and avoid some of the more controversial issues. But inevitably our interpretation will depend on a certain grasp of Kant's overall project.

We begin with Kant's explicitly stated assumption in the *Critique* that "we are in possession" of synthetic a priori knowledge and that "even the common understanding is never without it" (B3).[4] It is preeminently in the form of mathematics and "pure" natural science that we have this knowledge, and it is the latter, the science of nature, that is at issue in the Transcendental Analytic, to which the Transcendental Deduction belongs. In the Transcendental Deduction Kant often speaks of "empirical knowledge," also called "experience" (*Erfahrung, cf.* A93/B126, B147, B166), rather than a priori knowledge, as if *this* were the assumption on which his argument turns. In any case, it is clear that for Kant there can be no real empirical knowledge without a priori synthetic knowledge. And when he speaks of the "common understanding" (or common sense [*der gemeine Verstand*]), he seems to suggest that we have this knowledge, even synthetic a priori knowledge, without being scientists or being engaged in scientific theory. He might even be saying that we are "in possession" of this knowledge even if we are not explicitly aware that we have it.

In any case, in some sense we have this knowledge, and it is knowledge of sensible objects or of the sensible world. We know that Kant's ultimate question in the *Critique* concerns not mathematics or natural science but metaphysics, and that he defines metaphysics as knowledge—indeed, synthetic a priori knowledge—of God, freedom, and immortality (B7). But these objects of knowledge lie, according to Kant, beyond the sensible world. Kant is impressed by the skeptical attack on such metaphysical knowledge, especially Hume's attack. But he thinks that Hume's attack would also render impossible what is for Kant an obvious "fact" (*Faktum,* B128), namely our a priori knowledge of the sensible world. So if we can have a priori knowledge of the sensible world, why not also knowledge of the supersensible? The only way to answer this question is to find out *how* our knowledge of the sensible world is possible, before asking *whether* knowledge of the supersensible is possible.

Thus it is in answer to this question, how is our knowledge of the sensible world possible? that Kant begins the Transcendental Deduction by speaking of the subject (*Subjekt*) of knowledge and its "self-activity" (*Selbsttätigkeit*) or action (*Handlung*) of combining the manifold of representations (B130). And it is here that Kant asserts that "it must be possible for the 'I think' to accompany all my representations" (B131). Kant calls this "*pure apperception*, to distinguish it from empirical apperception." He also calls it "*original apperception*," and again "the *transcendental* unity of self-consciousness, in order to indicate the possibility of a priori knowledge arising from it" (B132).

I want to call attention to a certain shift of focus that occurs in the first two sections of the Deduction, one that is generally not commented upon by scholars. In the first (section 15), Kant seems to be asserting that experience requires "combination" and combination in turn requires an active subject that combines. The manifold of representations is given through the senses, but its combination or synthesis is not. Thus the supreme condition of the possibility of experience is that there *be* a subject that acts in this way. In this sense one could speak of a "transcendental subject"—though Kant does not do so here.[5]

But section 16, with its notion of pure apperception, while seeming simply to elaborate on what went before, actually changes its sense. From the context it is clear that Kant uses "apperception" to mean "self-consciousness." It is this "unity of self-consciousness" that is now called "transcendental," that is, a condition of the possibility of a priori knowledge. There is a shift of focus here because up to now Kant has been speaking of a consciousness of the sensible world, and now he is speaking of a *self*-consciousness. Of course the two go together, indeed necessarily so. But they are not the same. Kant is saying that, in knowing the sensible world, we must think of *ourselves* in a certain way—at least implicitly. He does not say that the "I think" *does* or *must* accompany all my representations, but only that it must be able to do so. Thus this implicit self-consciousness could always in principle be made explicit and expressed as "I think."

It is this "original," "synthetic," "pure" unity of apperception that is henceforth meant when Kant speaks of the supreme condition of the possibility of experience (B135). Thus I must revise my interpretation of section 15 where I said that the supreme condition is that there *be* a subject that acts in a certain way. Here Kant seems to be saying that the supreme condition is that we be *conscious of ourselves* in a certain way.

If Kant were simply affirming a link between consciousness and self-consciousness, his assertion might be seen as an extension of the link already found in Descartes and confirmed in Leibniz's account of the relation between perception and apperception. Kant does, after all, use Leibniz's term. The Leibnizian doctrine leads to grave difficulties, as many authors have pointed out; for one thing, it suggests an infinite regress of self-consciousnesses. And by continuing this line Kant would seem to confirm the view of Heidegger and others that he adheres to the substance theory of the self clearly propounded by these predecessors.[6]

But obviously Kant is saying something much more complicated than this. His distinction between pure and empirical apperception introduces a new element into the discussion. It is the former, and not the latter, that constitutes the supreme condition of our knowledge of the sensible world. What is crucial here is not just self-consciousness, but a certain *kind* of self-consciousness. Kant is saying that the possibility of experience requires that I be self-conscious in a special way. And it is in connection with this distinction between two forms of self-consciousness that any distinction between a transcendental subject and an empirical subject must be understood.

Thus in order to get at Kant's theory of the subject (or self), we must figure out what these two different modes of self-consciousness are. What I propose is to break the concept of self-consciousness down into its elements. One is the self *of which* I am conscious. How, that is, *as what or under what description*, does the self appear, is the self represented, in pure apperception, and how does it differ from the self that is represented in empirical apperception? The second element is the *consciousness* in which the self is thus represented. Kant has answers to both kinds of questions, in each case usually by contrasting the two forms of apperception, but it is not always easy to sort them out.

In the following I shall attempt, as far as possible, to pursue these questions separately. Thus I shall first consider "the self of which I am conscious" in both empirical and transcendental self-consciousness, and then "the consciousness of self," again in each of the two modes. I shall then be in a position to "reconstruct" the two forms of self-consciousness, putting the two sides back together, and to draw some conclusions from this investigation about the ultimate significance of Kant's theory of the self.

However, the procedure that I have just proposed may be subject to some serious objections before it even gets started. It may be thought that it rests on some dubious assumptions. The very idea of dividing self-consciousness into "self" and "consciousness of," even as abstractly considered parts of a conceptual whole, could be subject to two serious objections.

First, it could be argued that the proposed procedure takes self-consciousness as a consciousness whose *object* is "the self." But the expression "self-consciousness" can be understood in a completely reflexive sense, such that it must be understood as "consciousness of itself," or consciousness of consciousness. Thus each instance, episode, or act of consciousness would be aware of itself, but not of *a* "self" that is in some way other than itself, lying behind this particular episode, persisting or abiding before and after it, perhaps uniting it with other such episodes. Critics of Descartes's cogito argument have made the point that the self-certainty of thought does not extend beyond the particlar act and does not warrant the added assertion of the existence of the "ego."[7]

It is certainly true that the expression "self-consciousness" can be understood in this purely reflexive way, and the reproach to Descartes may be justified. But it is pretty clear that Kant does not understand self-consciousness in this way. In connection with it he frequently uses substantival expressions like "das Subjekt" (B130), "ein Selbst" (B134), and "das Ich" (B135); furthermore, the identity of the subject (Identität des Subjekts [B134]) through a multiplicity of diverse representations is clearly at issue when he speaks of self-consciousness. In transcendental apperception "bin ich mir meiner selbst . . . bewußt" (B157), he says, using an expression that unequivocally says that it is *myself* of which I am aware in this consciousness.

What is more, in this very passage Kant says that *what* I am consciousnes of here is "daß ich bin," *that* I am. Thus this self-consciousness seems to include the very same existence-claim about the ego put forward by Descartes. I shall have more to say about this later; for the moment it should be pointed out that Kant does not clai for this consciousness of my own existence the certainty attached to it by Descartes; in fact, as we shall see, for Kant it does not even have the status of knowledge. Thus the very features that made the cogito important for Descartes—its status as certain knowledge that could serve as a ground for other knowledge—seem to be lacking in Kant. If the well-known criticism of Descartes, mentioned above, concerns only the latter's epistemic claim, then Kant seems to escape it. But Kant is certainly claiming, contrary to the standard criticism, that being self-conscious means more than just "consciousness of consciousness" and embraces in some way the subject of consciousness as well.

But here a second prior objection could be raised. In what way am I conscious of myself in self-consciousness? It could be claimed that my way of setting up the question gets off on the wrong foot. I said above that I intended to ask: *As what*, that is, *under what description*, is the self *represented* in the two forms of self-consciousness? Speaking about self-consciousness as a form of representation, which subsumes its "object" under a description, that is, takes it *as* something, may miss

the point, at least in the case of transcendental apperception. It runs
the risk of depicting this form of consciousness as a conceptual grasp
akin to our cognition of other objects. In speaking of transcendental
self-consciouness, this may not be what Kant had in mind. It does not
accord well with his insistence on its being prior to, an accompaniment
of, all conceptual thought, a "bare consciousness" ("ein bloßes
Bewußtsein" [A346/B404]). Nor does it square with his claim that it
gives my existence, but no "determination" (*Bestimmung*) of my existence (B157n.).

Certain recent commentators have taken on this apparently non-
conceptual aspect of self-consciousness. R. Makkreel finds reasons (referring to the *Prolegomena* and the *Critique of Judgment*) for calling it a
feeling of self.[8] M. Frank argues that Kant, at least in some places, does
consider self-consciousness a subject-object relation, but should not
have done so, since he thereby perpetuated all the difficulties attaching
to the Cartesian-Leibnizian version of this self-relation. According to
Frank, Kant should have recognized that self-consciousness is "pre-
propositional," a form of familiarity or acquaintance (*Vertrautheit*) and
not a conceptual awareness.[9]

The best reply to this objection is to turn directly to the text, as I
shall directly do, and try to show that there is an "as-structure" or a
description to be found in what Kant says. Certainly he describes even
transcendental self-consciousness as involving a certain "representation" (*Vorstellung*) of myself (e.g., B132, B157). A concession to this
objection may be possible if we distinguish between an implicit or
unarticulated self-consciousness, on the one hand, and the explicit self-
consciousness, on the other, in which the "I think" not only may but
actually does accompany my representation. The disadvantage to this
suggestion is that Kant himself, to my knowledge, nowhere goes into
this distinction. In any case, it will turn out, when we turn later to the
second side of the relation, "the consciousness of self," that transcendental self-consciousness is indeed anything but a normal conceptual
grasp of an object, just as this objection claims. In spite of this it will
be possible to derive from it something like a description of "the self
of which I am conscious." It is to this that we now turn.

The Self of Which I Am Conscious:
Transcendental Versus Empirical

Let us turn first to transcendental, as opposed to empirical, apperception. When Kant speaks of the "I think" that must be able to accompany all my representations, he is indicating that in this "pure" self-

consciousness I am conscious of myself *as* thinking, not as walking, breathing, digesting, or in any of the other ways I might think of myself. But in German as in English, grammatically and conceptually, thinking requires an object: to think is to think *of* or *about* something or *that* something is the case.[10] In the terminology of a later period, thinking is intentional. Though Kant does not speak in these terms, it turns out that this feature of thinking is absolutely crucial to his project.

Of course, all thinking is intentional, but here Kant is interested in something quite specific, namely, our knowledge of the sensible world. The question here is: How is experience, that is, empirical knowledge, possible? Such knowledge requires that our thinking be linked with sense-representations or intuitions. But *how* are they linked? One might expect that, since thought requires an object, it is sense-representations that serve this function. It is they that our thought is *about*.

But this is precisely *not* what Kant is saying. In fact, his rejection of such a notion is a decisive aspect of his own doctrine and its relation to its predecessors.

Kant rejects the so-called way of ideas expressed notoriously by Locke when he said that the term "idea" "serves best to stand for whatsoever is the *object* of the understanding when a man thinks."[11] Kant indeed uses the term *Vorstellung*—usually rendered "representa-tion" in English—in a way that corresponds roughly to the term "idea" in English and its cognates in other languages, as used by Locke and other modern philosophers. And he believes that such representations, in the form of sensations or impressions (*Eindrücke*, A50/B74), are necessarily involved in our knowledge of the sensible world. But these representations are "a mere determination of the mind" (A50/B74. Compare A147/B242). And our knowledge of the sensible world is not about our mind or its contents or determination, but precisely about the sensible world. More precisely still, it is about objects in the sensible world. "An *object* is that in the concept of which the manifold of a given intuition is *united*" (B134). Our knowledge of the sensible world requires that we have such representations, indeed that they be given. But it also requires that, by their means, objects be thought. It requires, in other words, that a manifold of sense-intuition be taken to be united, not in the subject that has or receives them, but in an object.

Another way of putting this is to say that, in order to have knowl-edge of the sensible world, it is not enough that we *have* sense repre-sentations, we must also take them to *be* representations, that is, to present (*vor-stellen*) or stand for something beyond themselves. It might be thought that by calling them "representations" (*Vorstellungen*) Kant is suggesting that our sensations come with their referring function, so to speak, already attached.[12] Of course the older terms "ideas" and "impressions," as used by Kant's predecessors, convey the same thing. There is a sense in which sense-representations "refer" beyond themselves—two senses, in fact—but these are not conceptually tied to the notion of representation. First, representations are given, and so are presumably caused by something. Second, they are given in the "forms" of space and time, and thus stand in certain relations with others of their kind. But causal relations and spatiotemporal relations are not representational relations. Insofar as we claim to know something about the sensible world, we are claiming to know something other than our own sensations, which are merely the contents of our minds. Another way of expressing the "I think" that "accompanies" my representations would be to say, "I am representing an object."

These considerations explain why Kant goes on to say (section 18) that the transcendental unity of apperception is to be "entitled *objective*, and must be distinguished from the *subjective* unity of consciousness" (B139). This may seem curious, in view of Kant's earlier emphasis on the "possession" of representations by the "I": they "would not be one and all *my* representations, if they did not all belong to one self-consciousness" (B132). "Otherwise I should have as many-colored and diverse a self as I have representations" (B134). These remarks suggest that knowledge does require an a priori subjective unity, that is, one I to which the many representations belong. But now the emphasis is on their objective unity, by which Kant means "that unity through which all the manifold given in an intuition is united in a concept of the object" (B139). He even suggests here that the subjective unity is merely empirical. But the point is that transcendental apperception represents not merely the "I" in relation to its representations, but the "I" thinking objects through those representations.[13]

A question that jumps from the page here is: What does Kant mean by "through"? The answer is supposedly provided by the categories, which Kant has introduced earlier and which can be described as the a priori rules for combining sense-representations in such a way as to relate them to objects (A158/B197). Kant has listed the categories, deriving them from the table of judgments, since it is in judgments that all knowledge is embodied or expressed. But now he must explain how they function: "The explanation of the manner in which concepts can thus relate a priori to objects I entitle their transcendental deduction" (A85/B117). This is the relation between the so-called metaphysical and the transcendental deductions of the categories. The order of presentation might just as well have been reversed (which is roughly what I have done here). In any case, the details of Kant's theory of categories is less important for us than their relation to the unity of apperception.

As we have seen, Kant's insistence on the "objective" character of this self-consciousness indicates that in it, what is represented is not just the "I," and not just the "I" in relation to the sense-representations it has, and certainly not the sense-representations themselves, but the "I" in a thinking (or intentional) relation to the *objects* (and the relations among them) that make up the sensible world. It is the categories of substance (inherence and subsistence), causality, and community that are particularly important here. Through them, we stand in relation to the regulated and ordered realm that we call nature, of which our experience constitutes empirical knowledge. Now there can be no empirical knowledge without the a priori knowledge embodied in the categories. Empirical knowledge would always involve the application of the categories to particular manifolds in order to produce grounded judgments about the world. But these in turn require a consciousness of myself as making these judgments and through them knowing the world.

This is the place to contrast transcendental apperception with empirical apperception, with respect to how (that is, as what) the self is represented in self-consciousness. Kant distinguishes the objective or transcendental unity from "the *subjective* unity of consciousness, which is a *determination* of *inner sense*, through which the manifold of intuition for such [objective] combination is empirically given" (B139; interpolation by Kemp Smith). In this self-consciousness "I, as ... *thinking* subject, know myself as an object that is *thought*, in so far as I am given to myself ... yet know myself, like other phenomena, only as I appear to myself" (B155). The most obvious difference here is that empirical apperception affords not merely a self-consciousness but a self-knowledge. This is due to the fact that intuition (inner sense) provides material for "determining" this object. What is thus given to me here is presumably the manifold of sense-representations that belong *to* me, and perhaps the various thoughts I have and judgments I make as well. But these are all predicates or properties of me, arranged in temporal sequence, through which I acquire the status of a full-fledged object of knowledge, albeit only empirical knowledge, and only of myself as an appearance.

By contrast to the self of empirical apperception, which in this way becomes rich in content, the self of transcendental apperception may appear empty or bare. Some of Kant's language suggests this, as when he speaks of a "mere form of consciousness" (A382) or a mere "logical subject" (A350). He also describes transcendental apperception as being not even "a representation distinguishing a particular object, but a form of representation in general" (A346/B404). As I have already noted, such remarks may suggest that transcendental apperception yields no representation at all of the "I," and hence no description or "determination" for it. But these declarations are misleading in several respects. Kant is concerned to insist that no intuition is involved in transcendental apperception, and hence that none of the predicates that derive from intuition are available for characterizing the self. But it is not as if the self of transcendental apperception had no characteristics, no description at all. On the contrary, up to now we have been working out just what that description is, starting with the notion of *thinking*. Thinking has been further characterized in terms of acts of spontaneity through which combination occurs. And since Kant is dealing here with knowledge of the sensible world, that thinking has been further qualified: it is thought about objects in the world, thanks to the categories, and not about its own representations or intuitions.

Thus in the two forms of self-consciousness, it is hardly the case that the one presents the self as full, the other as entirely empty, of content or qualification. Instead we should speak of two senses of content, which correspond approximately to Husserl's distinction between the real (*reell*) or descriptive content and the intentional content of a conscious experience.[14] This distinction is roughly that between what an experience *is* and what it is *of*. Husserl believes that experiences cannot even be described or identified apart from their intentional content.[15] But we can also think of experiences in terms of mental predicates (sensations, feelings, thoughts) we attribute to the subject, thus characterizing the subject by their means; as opposed to construing them qua intentional with reference to their intentional content. This, I think, is the distinction Kant had in mind. In the one case (empirical self-consciousness) I am conscious of myself as an object with certain mental properties; in the other case (transcendental self-consciousness), I am conscious of myself *as* thinking, and thus in terms of *what it is* I am thinking—in this case the objects of the sensible world. In thinking of myself as thinking, I am of course attributing to myself what thinking is, namely the spontaneous activity of combining. I construe myself strictly in terms of the activity of thinking—specifically, thinking about the sensible world. The only sense in which I am empty or contentless is that, under this description, the only kind of content that counts is intentional content. And the intentional content of my thought is not in me or part of me but is "out there"—in the world. Thus transcendental apperception involves no characterization of me except that I am having these thoughts or making these judgments; beyond this there is no psychological description, no personal history, no grasp of the self as an object having such and such properties, and so forth.

This gives us an answer to our question: how—that is, as what or under what description—is the self represented in pure apperception? The answer is best articulated by contrast to empirical apperception. In the former the self is active, spontaneous, thinking, intentionally related to its objects and the world (*not* its representations); it is the "subject of the categories" (B422). In the latter the self is but a bearer of its representations, sensations, and thoughts (these being given through inner sense); it is an "object of the categories" (B422), the "soul" (B427). Here the self has personal identity, a history, that is an individuality that distinguishes it from other persons.

Granted that these two descriptions are very different from each other, are we entitled to speak of two different selves, a "transcendental" and an "empirical" self? Kant himself says they are "the same subject" (B155) but admits to great difficulty in reconciling the two descriptions. The real question is not whether there are two descriptions, of course, but whether they are incompatible descriptions. Only this would threaten or call into question the identity of the subject(s) being described. Are the two descriptions incompatible?

There are good reasons for saying that they are. In transcendental self-consciousness I represent myself as the spontaneous activity of thinking. This means that I take myself to be following rules or reasons, not to be causally determined in my activity. As H. Allison puts it, "[T]aking something as a reason for belief, like adopting an end or deciding on a course of action, is not something that we can *consider ourselves* caused to do.... For Kant..., the reasons for one's belief cannot be regarded as a set of causes producing it.[16] Spontaneity in this sense is of course something that no natural object can have. Anything that can be given in intuition, and thus become an object of empirical knowledge, must be subject to the category of causality; that is, it is not just an isolated object but belongs in a regulated way to the other objects and events that make up nature. This is how the self is represented in *empirical* apperception. It is given in inner sense, it is an object of empirical knowledge, and thus it must belong to nature, that is, be a part of it and subject to its laws. In empirical self-consciousness, even if I represent myself as having thoughts as well as sensations and perhaps other mental properties, I can have no intuition, Kant says, of the spontaneity itself (B157n.). Thus presumably in empirical self-consciousness I am not represented as a spontaneous or self-active being *(selbsttätiges Wesen)*. How can two descriptions be of the same entity if one description makes it spontaneous or self-active and the other non-spontaneous, non-self-active?

But this incompatibility is insignificant compared to that which emerges when we consider not the spontaneity but the intentionality of the thinking subject. In pure apperception, I represent myself as intentionally related to objects of thought—in the present case, objects of empirical knowledge. But these objects are such, thanks to the categories, as to make up a whole realm or system of lawful interconnections, which we have been calling the sensible world and which Kant calls nature.[17] Implicitly it is not just individual objects, but all of nature, which constitutes the "intentional object" of empirical knowledge. Now if there is a conceptual requirement belonging to the concept of intentionality, that we distinguish consciousness from its object, or in this case knowledge from the object known, then conceptually the subject of knowledge is distinct from nature. In other words, the knowledge of nature requires, as a condition of its possibility, that we distinguish ourselves from nature.

To this conceptual or formal distinctness Kant adds distinctness of yet a different sort. The relation of my thought to nature is not just one of thought to its object. Thanks to the categories, the laws that constitute nature are laws prescribed ("as it were" [*gleichsam*]) by the understanding (B159) that stands under the transcendental unity of apperception. Thus, in knowing the sensible world I am represented not only as distinct from it but also as prescribing laws to it. It would seem that I am therefore not subject to its laws but that they are subject to me.

Thus, the incompatibility of the two descriptions is apparently complete. It is not even a question of two incompatible descriptions of a putative *object*. Only empirical apperception gives us a description of an *object* that exists in the world together with other objects. Transcendental apperception, by contrast, represents an "I" that is not part of the (sensible) world at all, by virtue of standing conceptually (that is, intentionally) over against or distinct from it, and by virtue of possessing a property (spontaneity) that rules out its inclusion in the world.

This is not, however, to say that the "transcendental" subject could be described without reference to the world, or even simply as being excluded from the world. For both subjects can be correctly described only "with reference" to the sensible world. Rather, it is a question of two incompatible sorts of relations to the world—if we are prepared to use the word "relation" loosely enough: the empirical self stands in a relation of inclusion and thus a part-whole relation to the world; the transcendental self stands in an intentional or subject-object relation to the world.

Thus we see that "the self of which I am conscious" in transcendental self-consciousness is radically different from the self of which I am conscious in empirical self-consciousness. One is part of, and the other is *not* part of, the sensible world: how could they be more different than that? Is talk of a "transcendental ego" and an "empirical ego" then justified? In order to answer this we must pass to the second part of the question, concerning the nature of the consciousness in which the self represents itself under the descriptions I have been discussing.

Kant and His Predecessors: The Problem of Skepticism

Before we do that, it will be useful to look at Kant's description of the "transcendental" self in light of his relation to his modern forerunners. I have already noted that Kant rejects the "way of ideas" as articulated by Locke. Knowledge of the empirical world requires that the mind be related not merely to its own "ideas" (sense representations) but rather, through those ideas, to objects. Kant is not, it seems clear, asking *whether* the mind is so related, but *how*. To ask "whether" would be to attempt to refute skepticism regarding our knowledge of nature. A long tradition of commentators has taken Kant to be doing just that,[18] placing him in a direct line with Descartes, who is thought to have inaugurated modern philosophy by defending the new Galilean science against skepticism. Descartes is judged to have failed, as Hume and others showed, and Kant is depicted as someone who arrives on the scene to save the day and defeat skepticism once and for all.

But it is hard to square this view of Kant's task with the fact that he unequivocally affirms that "we are in possession" of such knowledge. He seems not to agree with Descartes that scientific knowledge must look to philosophy for a warrant it is incapable of providing for itself. He notes that in his day "the study of nature has entered on the secure path of a science, after having for so many centuries been nothing but a process of merely random groping (*ein bloßes Herumtappen*)" (Bxiv). His view seems to be that the great advances in science since Descartes' time provide it with all the warrant it needs.

It may be that commentators of the *Critique* ascribe to its author the intention to defeat skepticism because they cannot imagine what else he might be doing. Besides, since skepticism had not yet been defeated, what else would any self-respecting philosopher do? Further, Kant expresses great admiration for Hume while disagreeing with him. Surely he could not be responding to Hume by simply taking for granted what Hume cast in doubt. If Kant is *not* out to defeat skepticism, what is he doing?

Kant is, to be sure, crucially concerned with skepticism, but it is skepticism about metaphysics, not natural science, that inspires the *Critique of Pure Reason*, as its first pages show. As we have noted, Kant's question could be stated as follows: if we can have a priori knowledge of the sensible world (and we do), why not of the supersensible world as well? The answer is to be found by asking how we have the knowledge we do, and this requires that the faculty of knowledge, and the subject of knowledge, be characterized in a certain way. It is this task, rather than a supposed refutation of skepticism about science, that requires that the "way of ideas" be rejected.

And yet it cannot be correct to say that Kant is completely unconcerned with skepticism about our knowledge of the sensible world. This would be to say that Kant simply takes as established everything that Descartes and Hume placed in doubt. But the problem of skepticism arose out of these philosophers' conception of what it means to have knowledge. Their idea of possessing knowledge of the "real world," expressed in Kantian terms, was to have cognition of things in themselves, that is, of things that are fully independent of us. When Kant stipulates at the beginning of the *Critique* that "we are in possession" of a priori knowledge, he cannot mean knowledge in this sense, though he does not say so at the time. As he tells us later, if we begin with this idea of knowledge (that of "transcendental realism"), we will surely end in skepticism. "After wrongly supposing that objects of the senses, if they are to be external, must have an existence by themselves, and independently of the senses, [the realist] finds that, judged from this point of view, all our sensuous representations are inadequate to establish their reality" (A369). The transcendental realist, unwittingly in league with the skeptic, sets up an alternative: either our knowledge is of things in themselves or it is "merely subjective," that is, not really knowledge at all. But this is an alternative Kant refuses to accept. For him it is obvious that, at least in science and mathematics, our knowledge is, in some important sense, *not* merely subjective. But if we define it as a relation between representations and things in themselves, we must conclude that it is. It is the conception of knowledge that must be questioned.[19]

Seen in this light, Kant's attitude toward skepticism, in relation to our knowledge of the sensible world, is more complex than it seems.

It is true that he does not set out to refute the skeptic; but at the same time he does not regard the skeptic's problem simply as solved in favor of scientific knowledge. For that would be to accept the way the problem is set up by the skeptic and the "transcendental realist" together. We might say that, just as Kant's book is a work *about* but not *of* metaphysics, so it is also about, but not an attempt to solve, the problem of skepticism. He is addressing himself, not merely to the skeptics, but to all parties in the debate. And it is their general conception of knowledge that is being questioned, first with respect to the sensible world. Thus Kant is more concerned with what such knowledge is rather than whether we have it. In this sense his question would be prior to that of the skeptic. The *what* question is, if you will, a question of essence rather than existence, of possibility rather than actuality.

This, then, is what Kant means by asking after the possibility of mathematics, natural science, and metaphysics. And this interpretation of Kant's stated question "how is synthetic *a priori* knowledge possible?" permits us to understand better his complex but very close relationship to the skeptical problem and to his predecessors generally. He thinks they have misunderstood what knowledge is, that is, what its essential features are, in mathematics, science, and metaphysics. Once this *what* question is satisfactorily answered, Kant thinks, then it will be clear *whether* we have knowledge in these domains; and he obviously believes that we do have it in the first two and do not in the third. But his belief would be justified in essential, not factual terms. For what knowledge is—or would be, or is supposed to be—in traditional metaphysics turns out to be something like a round square. There can be no instances of it. In this sense the skeptical question in its broadest sense would eventually be addressed and even answered. But it would not be answered in the terms set up by Kant's predecessors. So Kant's primary task is a major overhaul of those terms.

What are those terms? We have seen that they are essentially two: the mind and its representations, on the one side, and things in themselves, on the other. Thus are the subject and object of knowledge portrayed. Kant addresses himself to the problem of knowledge in a way that requires that both terms of this conception be radically revised; and he addresses them more or less in this order—though inevitably the two sides cannot really be disentangled. A revised conception of knowledge itself will make it possible and necessary to conceive of the object of knowledge other than as thing in itself. This is where Kant's theory of appearances comes in, and ultimately his notion of transcendental idealism. But these depend on a radical reassessment of what knowledge is or would be, first in relation to the sensible world. This is what leads Kant to a theory of mind and a theory of the subject.

The "way of ideas" is a characterization not only of the knowing process but also implicitly of the knowing subject. And in this sense it is held not only by Locke and the empiricists but by the rationalists as well. It consists in the view that the mind is a thing (*res*) that has certain properties, even if these properties may be thoughts, ideas, or representations rather than other kinds of properties. But Kant affirms, as we have seen, that the mind must not merely have representations, it must take them to be representations; it must at the very least take them to refer beyond themselves. But the tradition has no place in its theory of mind for this act of taking. This act is nothing other than the "I think" whereby I relate my representations to objects by means of concepts.

This implicit criticism of the "way of ideas" is the first volley in Kant's attack on the metaphysics of the subject. Prior to his explicit attack on rational psychology, Kant is saying that his predecessors think of the mind simply as having its ideas in the same way that a thing, according to traditional metaphysics, has its properties. It becomes a substance alongside other substances in the world. But in order to account for the knowledge we have (that of the sensible world), the self must be charracterized, as we have seen, as distinct from the world, as prescribing laws to the world, as spontaneous, not caused. Above all we must start with the mind's relation to objects and to the world, and not expect to establish it somehow after the fact.

But what is the status of this attack on the metaphysics of the subject? Is Kant not merely rejecting one metaphysical theory of the self in order to replace it with another theory? In order to answer this, we must now move to the second part of our main question.

The Consciousness of Self: Transcendental and Empirical

As we have seen, it is a peculiar kind of self-consciousness, not simply a peculiar kind of self, which according to Kant is the supreme condition of our knowledge of the sensible world. Transcendental apperception is peculiar in that it characterizes or describes the self in a quite distinctive way, as we have seen. But it is also peculiar in how it does this; and in this it differs from empirical self-consciousness. What sort of consciousness is involved in each case? Many of Kant's most difficult remarks in the Transcendental Deduction are designed to answer this question, and to these we must now turn.

We have seen that transcendental self-consciousness is not an intuition of self. We do indeed have an intuition of self, in the form of inner sense. Here the self can become an object of knowledge, subject of course to the categories, and accordingly given as an appearance, not as a thing in itself. But this self-consciousness is empirical, not a priori; it is an instance of experience, not a condition of the possibility of experience and hence not transcendental. It represents the self, with its mental properties, as part of the world.

Describing this empirical form of self-consciousness and self-knowledge is not without its problems, as Kant admits. He calls it a paradox (B152) and goes to some lengths to make sense of the idea that the self could be inwardly affected by, and thus in a relation of passive reception to, its own activity (B153–156).

But the description of transcendental self-consciousness is no less difficult. Here I am conscious of myself "not as I appear to myself, nor as I am in myself, but only that I am. This *representation* is a *thought*, not an *intuition*" (B157)—or more precisely, a *thinking*, not an *intuiting*: "ein *Denken*, nicht ein *Anschauen*." I have inner sense, which permits me to "determine" (*bestimmen*) my existence, that is, apply predicates to it through judgments, so that it becomes a determined or determinate object. But

> since I do not have another self-intuition which gives the *determining* (*das Bestimmende*) in me (I am *merely conscious* [my alteration, my emphasis:DC] of the spontaneity of it) . . . I cannot determine my existence as that of a self-active being; all that I can do is represent to myself the spontaneity of my thought . . . But it is owing to this spontaneity that I entitle myself an *intelligence*. (B157n.)

Thus we have a self-consciousness in which the self is indeed represented, even thought, as spontaneous, but not intuited, since spontaneity cannot be intuited. In the Paralogisms Kant first speaks of the "I think" as a "judgment" involving a "concept"—indeed a concept that ought to be counted among the categories (A341/B399). But a few pages later he says of the representation "I" that "we cannot even say that it is a concept, but merely that it is a bare consciousness [*ein bloßes Bewußtsein*] that accompanies all concepts" (A346/B404).

These remarks suggest that the transcendental unity of apperception is not only not intuitive, it is not conceptual either. In a recent work, as I noted earlier, R. Makkreel links it to a special Kantian version of the notion of *feeling*.[20] In a study whose main focus is the *Critique of Judgment*, Makkreel asserts that the idea of *life* "pervades the entire structure" of that work, not as a biological notion but as a prior "feeling of mental life" from which the biological derives its meaning (p. 103). Understood in a non- or pre-empirical way, this feeling of life not only unites the aesthetic and teleological sides of the third Critique, but also links up with "the transcendental conditions of human experience and action" in general (p. 105). Thus Makkreel is able to project his findings in the *Critique of Judgment* back onto the first Critique and the consciousness of the "I think." This is facilitated by a passage in the *Prolegomena* in which the transcendental consciousness of self is described as "nothing more than the *feeling* of an existence without the least concept."[21] This feeling of the existence of the transcendental ego can thus be "pure and formal," and "may be none other than the pure aesthetic feeling of life" that in the third Critique is called the "bare consciousness of existence." "It is the transcendental feeling of spontaneity (the *actus* of life)," says Makkreel, "that corresponds to the spontaneity of the intellect (the *actus* 'I think')" (p. 105).

Makkreel's proposal is appealing in several respects. It casts a new light on the difficult notion of transcendental apperception in the first Critique, and at that same time links it to Kant's later work, drawing from the *Prolegomena* passage undeniable support for doing so. Another important link is the term "spontaniety," which provides for something common between the earlier "I think" and the later "feeling of life." Above all, this proposal furnishes a way of acknowledging the distinctive character of the transcendental "I think," against any tendency to assimilate it to ordinary conceptual thought or interpret it as a judgment that stands on the same level with other judgments.[22]

The only disadvantage of Makkreel's proposal is that it seems hard to square self-consciousness as "feeling" with the heavily "conceptual" context of the *Critique of Pure Reason* in which the doctrine of transcendental apperception is developed. That is, the questions addressed in that work (that is, how mathematics, science, and metaphysics are possible) are different from those of the *Critique of Judgment* (aesthetic and teleological judgments). Still, Makkreel stresses that the "feeling" Kant has is mind is "pure" and not linked to the senses (p. 104), and that the conception of "life" in question is, as we noted, non-vitalistic or at least non-biological.

The important point is that transcendental self-consciousness, while it may be expressed in the judgment "I think," is not an instance of the "ordinary" employment of concepts in judgment. But it is, at least in the first Critique, intimately linked with the ordinary employment of concepts and is to that extent conceptual. This is, I think, perfectly compatible with Makkreel's proposal. Where Kant stresses the non- or pre-conceptual character of transcendental self-conciousness, he wants to distinguish it from the normal employment of concepts, whose purpose is to make judgments about objects. Any such judgment, even if it attempts to be *about* the "I", would presuppose, rather than simply express, the transcendental "I think." Hence, we could "only revolve in a perpetual circle, since any judgment upon [the "I"] has always already made use of its representation" (A346/B404). But this is just a way of saying that transcendental self-consciousness is not a direct, face-to-face awareness of myself, but a secondary or oblique reference that is always parasitic on a first-order judgment. *Empirical* self-consciousness is a direct awareness, possibly expressed in a judgment about myself. *Transcendental* self-consciousness is what I have when making judgments about anything at all: God, the world, or even myself. This is the "accompanying" role of the "I think." And this is also another way of noting the intentional character of this representation of the "I think:" I am aware of it only through its intentional content, that is, what it is of or about.

Thus there is an important sense in which transcendental apperception is non-conceptual or pre-conceptual; but it is directly tied to the conceptual as the condition of the possibility of all employment of concepts, including any employment that might refer to the self. It takes the form of a judgment ("I think") and even employs concepts, but it occurs only as a concomitant feature of some other judgment or judgments. C. Evans suggests that it be described as a judgment of indirect discourse (I think that *p*).[23]

Are There Two Selves?

I have now said enough about "the self of which I am conscious" and "the consciousness of self" in transcendental and in empirical apperception to be able to return to the main questions with which we started and that have arisen in the course of our inquiry.

I began by asking whether Kant's philosophy is a metaphysics of the subject. This question is closely tied to that of whether Kant is claiming that there are not one but two subjects, an empirical and a transcendental. Let me address this second question before returning to the first. What can we say about this now? Are there two subjects? Do they both exist in the same sense? Is there any way in which they are still the same subject?

This may be the place to consider one version of the relation between the transcendental and the empirical subject that we have not considered so far, but that has suggested itself to many readers of Kant, and is thought to provide a solution to the question of "two subjects." This is the idea that the transcendental ego is just the pure form or concept, the Platonic essence of any subject at all—egoness, as it were—while the empirical subject is the particular person that I am, with my history, personality, and so forth. This is suggested when Kant speaks of the "I think" as "not a representation distinguishing a particular object, but a form of representation in general (*eine Form derselben überhaupt*)" (A346/B404), and when he says, "I thereby represent myself to myself neither as I am nor as I appear to myself. I think myself only as I do any object in general (*überhaupt*) from whose mode of intuition I abstract" (B429). And in the *Prolegomena*, in a similar context, he speaks of "consciousness in general" [*Bewußtsein überhaupt*].[24] On this interpretation, transcendental and empirical subjects would simply stand in a type-token relationship and thus on two completely different logical or ontological levels. It would make no more sense to speak of two subjects or selves than it does to speak of two dogs when considering Fido and the concept "dog." Instead, in one form of self-consciousness I would consider the general concept of which I am an instance, in the other myself as an instance of that concept.

This interpretation may seem reinforced by one of the things I said earlier in this chapter about the difference between the transcendental and the empirical: only the latter, by providing me with predicates or what Kant calls "determinations" (psychological characteristics, a personal history, etc.), can serve to differentiate me from others. The former, since it apparently concerns only what I share with all subjects, seems capable of offering no such individuation.

From here it may seem a short step to the Averroistic conception that the Transcendental Ego (capitalized, of course) is One, while all the empirical egos are many. Since some version of this notion was current among Kant's idealist successors (Schelling, Fichte, and Hegel), it may be thought that they were simply building on an idea already found—or at least foreshadowed—in Kant. Of course this would require a tie-in with the Platonic problem of self-predication (the form of man is a man, the form of egoness is an Ego), which hardly seems present in Kant.

In any case, such a conception is ruled out by our findings so far. First, Kant's language indicates, as we have already seen, that in transcendental as well as empirical self-consciousness I am conscious of *myself* (cf. "bin ich mir meiner selbst ... bewußt" [B157]), not of some empty concept. Indeed, it is of my own *existence* ("daß ich bin" [B157]) that I am conscious. At best one could say that in the two forms of self-consciousness I am aware of myself, but in one case I "abstract" (cf. B429) from everything but what I share with all others. Thus I would be conscious of myself strictly qua thinker in general (*überhaupt*), not qua *this* thinker of *these* thoughts, with this particular history, and so forth.

But this will not do either. As we have seen, while the subject of transcendental apperception does not have "determinations" in the sense that the empirical subject does, it is not without characteristics. It is characterized precisely as spontaneous, as thinking, as intentional (on our interpretation), most important, in these respects it differs radically from the self of empirical apperception. It is evident that Kant is giving us not a type-token distinction but rather two separate types or descriptions, which may even be incompatible with each other. Whether this in turn requires that there be two tokens, two selves, is the question we still have to consider.

Nevertheless, the question of individuation is an interesting one in this context, and some reflection will show why, apart from the Kantian passages quoted above, the Averroistic solution might suggest itself. If it is true that the empirical ego provides for the properties that distinguish me from other persons, is it the case that the transcendental ego has no individuation? Some passages from Fichte's "Second Introduction to the Science of Knowledge" (1797)[25] may prove instructive here. In order to separate the issues of selfhood (*Ichheit*) and individuality, Fichte uses a homey example, which I will paraphrase here: If you call out in the dark, "Who's there?" and I reply, "It is I," I mean I, David Carr, and not someone else. By contrast, if someone is sewing a button on my shirt and accidentally sticks me with a pin, I may say, "Hey, that's *me* you're sticking," and mean something quite different (pp. 73f). As Fichte puts it, "When I say that I am that which thinks in this thinking, do I then merely posit myself over against other persons outside me? Or do I not rather contrast myself with everything that is thought?" (p. 73).

Fichte's point is valid, and it is interesting to note that it applies to an experience like feeling a pain as well as to conceptual thought. In these experiences I am conscious of myself as the "ultimate" subject from which everything else is distinguished. "Everything else" can be at most actual and possible *objects* of experience, never the *subject* in the sense that I am for myself. Some of these objects can of course be subjects for themselves, and then I have to distinguish myself as individual from them as individuals. But they retain their status of objects *for me* in the process. It is in this latter role—the I *for whom*—that I am what Kant calls a transcendental subject. And in this role the problem or issue of individuality simply does not arise, does not enter in, is not relevant.

Unfortunately, Fichte draws the wrong conclusion when he says, "This self, however, is selfhood in general" ("Dieses Ich aber ist die Ichheit überhaupt") (p. 73). But it is not clear why he thinks generality should enter in here, much less universality. I am still conscious of myself in this mode, even if in a different way from my distinguishing myself from others. It is not "selfhood" that feels pain or makes a judgment, it is I myself. What corresponds to, and is distinguished from, selfhood is worldhood, or objectivity ("objecthood," "thing-hood," etc.). These concepts are treated in philosophical discussions like the one you are reading now. But what I feel and experience is not worldhood or thinghood but things and objects—and persons—and the world to which they belong. And indeed, if I do go on to distinguish between worldhood and worldly things, or even between selfhood and particular selves, it is I, not selfhood, who does this. Concepts or ideas are *also* objects of which I am conscious.

And in being conscious of them I also distinguish myself from them. Hegel has a description—or definition—of consciousness that is apt here: Consciousness "*distinguishes* something from itself to which it at the same time *relates* itself."[26] It is the self-consciousness implicit in this notion of consciousness that best approximates, I think, what Kant has in mind. It is the "self" that distinguishes itself from anything of which it could possibly be conscious, particular or general. Thus it is itself neither general nor particular but *prior* to any distinction between the general and the particular. Perhaps we could say that, like the world from which it distinguishes itself, it is singular, at least as it functions in this level of self-consciousness. There is only one world, and while there are many selves, there is only one *myself*.

We can now return to the question of whether Kant is claiming that in addition to this "transcendental" self there is, for each of us, a completely different "empirical" self. We have seen that there are good reasons for saying that Kant does claim this, since he proposes two radically different, indeed incompatible descriptions of the self. We have also noted that his theory of the subject addresses itself to the meta-physics of the subject of his predecessors, that is, the conception of the subject that was involved in the debate over skepticism in modern philosophy. Kant implicitly traces this debate to the substantial con-ception of the self presupposed by the "way of ideas," and proposes his "transcendental" subject as a way not of answering the skeptic, but of changing the terms of the debate. Is he then not countering one metaphysics of the subject with another?

We can begin our answer to this question by repeating what we said in commenting on the first pages of the Transcendental Deduction. While Kant at first seems to say that experience (empirical knowledge) requires that there *be* a subject of a certain sort, he actually says instead that experience requires that we be conscious of ourselves in a certain way. It is "apperception" or "self-consciousness" that is described as pure, original, and transcendental, that is, as supreme condition of the possibility of experience.

But, as we have seen, Kant does not speak merely of self-consciousness, but of a special kind, which he describes in some detail and distinguishes from another kind, namely empirical self-consciousness. Although Kant sometimes speaks of transcendental apperception as "mere" or even "bare" self-consciousness, in fact it has a distinctive character that can be analyzed, as I have tried to do here, with reference to its representation of the self and with reference to the kind of consciousness it is. In transcendental apperception I am not only conscious of myself; I represent myself—implicitly, at least—as a self of a certain sort, namely, as spontaneous, as intelligence, as intentional, as legislating to nature and hence as not subject to or part of the sensible world. Thus transcendental self-consciousness carries with it a distinctive description of the self that is different from the description of myself that is coupled, according to Kant, with my empirical self-consciousness.

Is There a Transcendental Subject?

We have, then, a transcendental description of the self—or, perhaps, a description of the transcendental self. But is there such a self?

Kant says, in a passage already quoted, that in transcendental apperception I am conscious that I am (B157), that in the "I think" "existence is already given thereby" (B157n.). But when it comes to "determining" my existence, that is, giving it a description as an object to be known, I can know myself only under the description provided by inner sense, and this is very different from the description attaching to transcendental apperception. Hence, in empirical self-consciousness I not only describe myself in a certain way (as subject of mental predicates, as part of the world, as causally determined); I also know myself as such or to be such, thanks to inner sense. In transcendental apperception, by contrast, I cannot *know* myself to be as I am described (spontaneous, etc.) but am only *conscious* of myself as such.

This is decisive for our question of whether there is a transcendental self. If the condition of the possibility of experience were that I know myself as spontaneous, intentional, and so forth, then we would be justified in saying that the fact that there is experience proves that I am such. But the possibility of experience requires only that I am conscious of myself as such, not that I know myself as such.

In fact, we can say equally that experience also requires (though in a somewhat different sense of "requires") that I take myself to be an empirical subject; and *that* self-consciousness goes further by delivering the evidence that I am indeed such. Thus the "fact," as Kant calls it, of our synthetic a priori knowledge of the sensible world requires that I describe myself in two incompatible ways, but only in one case, that of empirical self-consciousness, do I know myself to be as I am described.

If this is so, we can hardly speak of two subjects. We may have two self-descriptions, but only one of them can acquire ontological status, thanks to the complicated mechanism of inner sense. Lacking this ontological status, what is the other description, that of the "transcendental subject," but a fiction? Just as I can describe myself in imagination as free of gravity, so that I can soar with the birds, so I can describe myself as free of worldly causality generally, and even as the author or legislator of its order. But it does not follow that I really am so. "Fiction" is of course the word favored by Hume to describe "the notion of a *soul*, and *self* and *substance*" lying behind our changing perceptions,[27] and the term has been taken up recently by a contemporary Humean as well. D. Dennett proposes that the self is a fiction comparable to the "center of gravity" we impute to objects. The center of gravity is not a thing in the world, not real in any usual sense. But it is a convenient and useful notion in dealing with things.[28] Hume is saying much the same about the concept of self. Kant is notoriously opposed to Hume's fictionalism, both in this context and others. But how, in the end, can he avoid such a conclusion, especially as regards the "transcendental self"?

The first thing to be said is that, if the transcendental subject is a fiction, it is a necessary fiction. The word "fiction" is closely linked, in use and in etymology, with feigning or pretending and is thus associated with the freedom of our imagination or fantasy. Even Hume admits that his "fictions" are not mere whimsy, but the most he will allow is that they are useful or convenient. Kant's claim about the transcendental subject is much stronger. Empirical knowledge requires that we represent ourselves in this way, namely as distinct from and not subject to the causal order of the sensible world we know. Insofar as we have knowledge of the sensible world (and we do), we are not free *not* to consider ourselves in this way—though of course we are equally constrained to think of ourselves in the incompatible role of object in the sensible world.

Thus while the two descriptions differ in epistemic status—one is knowledge, the other is not—and in the ontological status that seems to follow, they do not differ with respect to constraint. Both are required; in fact, both are required, though in different ways, by the same thing: empirical knowledge.

Another sense attached to the word "fiction" is that it refers to something we consciously take to be non-existent, and in doing so we implicitly contrast it with what does exist. Fictional characters in plays and novels have the most elaborate descriptions, and we can become acquainted with their personalities as if they lived lives of their own; but we do not for a moment think that they exist or ever existed. Kant says, by contrast, that in transcendental apperception I am conscious of my own existence; there is no suggestion that the self of which I am conscious, in this form of self-consciousness, is a self I take *not* to exist.

To be sure, if we identified "what exists" with the sensible world, we would find it hard to avoid this conclusion, since the transcendental self has been explicitly described as not belonging to that world, as part to whole, but as being distinct from it, as subject to intentional object, and as not being subject to its laws. But this identification of what exists with the sensible world is one that Kant refuses to make. This is where his notorious concept of the thing in itself enters in. To exist as a natural object in the sensible world is to exist as what Kant calls an "appearance." Existing in this way entails being subject to the categories and the laws they prescribe. But existing in this way is not, or may not be, the only way of existing. While I cannot *know* myself to exist as a transcendental subject, I *may* yet exist in this way, not as appearance but as thing in itself.

We have now entered the domain of the Transcendental Dialectic, particularly the Paralogisms of Pure Reason and the Third Antinomy. The arguments of these sections are directed against two opposed adversaries. The former is addressed to those who would derive an a priori metaphysics of the subject (or "rational psychology") from the "sole text" of transcendental apperception, "I think" (A343/B401), and draw conclusions about the immortality of the soul. "The unity of consciousness, which underlies the categories, is here mistaken for an intuition of the subject as object, and the category of substance is then applied to it" (B421). The point here is the one I have already made: though I must *take* myself to be in a sense non-worldly, I cannot know myself to be so.

The Third Antinomy, by contrast, is addressed to those materialists or idealists who would draw the conclusion directly opposed to that of the rational psychologists. The materialist position would be as follows: since I can *know* myself only as worldly, that is, as part of the sensible world and hence as subject to its universal causality, I must conclude that I am not or cannot be non-worldly in the sense of the spontaneous, intentional, and free subject that I take myself to be. Kant is here linking the freedom of the moral agent with the spontaneity of the subject of empirical knowledge (see A546/B574 and ff.). Whether moral freedom and epistemological spontaneity can be equated in this sense or not,[29] we have established at least that the transcendental self is free in the sense of being not subject to, but subject of, worldly causality. Now Kant is saying that although I can know myself only as causally determined, I may yet exist (as thing in itself) as transcendental subject. Kant believes that his concept of transcendental idealism, with its distinction between appearances and things in themselves, permits us to conclude that "freedom is at least not *incompatible with* nature" (A558/B586).

Many readers, even some of Kant's admirers, find him at best unpersuasive here. Not least among the difficulties attached to the idea of transcendental idealism and that of the thing in itself is that it loosens one of our most sacred conceptual bonds, that between knowing and being, and thus threatens a kind of conceptual anarchy. Kant insists that we have empirical knowledge, yet it is knowledge only of appearances. This implication is especially abhorrent to those who see Kant as an opponent of skepticism, since this doctrine seems to land him squarely among the skeptics. We have seen that it is a gross oversimplification to see Kant in this role, but it is not our intention here to enter into a general debate about transcendental idealism, much less to defend Kant on this point.[30] It is quite possible, however, to present a plausible reading of his views, at least as they affect his theory of the subject. Such a reading is found in the work of G. Prauss and H. Allison.[31] According to this view, appearances are neither mere appearances, nor a separate set of objects different from things in themselves. As Allison puts it:

> At the transcendental level, ... the distinction between appearances and things in themselves refers primarily to two distinct ways in which things (empirical objects) can be 'considered': either in relation to the conditions of human sensibility (space and time), and thus as they 'appear,' or independently of these conditions, and thus as they are 'in themselves.'(p. 8)

One commentator who has argued persuasively against the view that Kant is defending science against skepticism, R. C. S. Walker, writes: "Strawson and others like him start out with the expectation that [Kant's] transcendental arguments can be used to establish something about what the world must be like, and not just about what we must take it to be like, if we are to have experience of it." Walker believes that "the conclusions most [Kantian] arguments can be expected to establish are about ourselves and our beliefs, not about the world."[32] Suppose we take Kant's theory of the categories, causality in particular, as a theory of what we must take the world to be like, if we are to have experience (i.e., empirical knowledge) of it. This makes universal causality something like an assumption about the world, permitting us to subsume empirical regularities under it or, if you will, a rule for interpreting empirical regularities, namely, as instances of universal causality. We can "know" these regularities in the sense that, in line with our assumption, we attribute them to the world, not to our own subjective impressions. But universal causality is not itself something we know in this way, it is only something we assume. (Of course, this would not square with Kant's claim that "every alteration has a cause" is one of the items of synthetic [a priori] knowledge we possess.)

This would accord, at least in part, with Hume's important discovery, with which Kant heartily agreed, that causality, in the sense of necessary connection, is not something we encounter in experience. For Hume it thus acquires, like the concept of the self, and like Dennett's center of gravity, the status of one of those useful and convenient fictions. Again Kant would object to this terminology, and for the same reasons as before: the belief in universal causality is necessary—this is probably why Kant would call it not merely a belief but knowledge—and is hence certainly not the consciousness of something we implicitly believe not to exist. But Kant would probably agree that if the transcendental self is a fiction, then universal causality is no less a fiction, and for similar reasons: both are required for experience to be possible.

If universal causality has this status—let me revert to the term "assumption"—what are the consequences for our "knowledge" of objects in the sensible world? It is true that they are given in sensation, but

what we know about them turns out to be either a priori assumption—
they are objects in space and time that are strictly regulated causally—or
empirical claims dependent on this assumption—this regularity we observe is an instance of that strict regularity we assume to be there. Thus
our "knowledge" of the sensible world depends heavily on such assumptions, and the conceptual connection between knowing and being
can only mean that the world is as we take it to be, granted these
assumptions. It is not quite correct to say, with Walker, that Kant's
arguments are in the end only about "ourselves and our beliefs." They
are indeed about the world; but they are about the world qua intentional
object, or, as Walker himself says, the world as we (must) take or
assume it to be. But of course we make these assumptions, and there
is no sense in which they can be justified. The Transcendental Deduction, as I have said, only shows how the categories work, but

> this peculiarity of our understanding, that it can produce *a priori* unity
> of apperception solely by means of the categories, and only by such and
> so many, is as little capable of further explanation as why we have just
> these and no other functions of judgment, or why space and time are
> the only forms of our possible intuition. (B146)

This interpretation of Kant's transcendental idealism has the effect
of rectifying the "ontological imbalance" we thought we had discovered
earlier between the "transcendental self" and the "empirical self," and
of placing them on the same or very similar footing. I do not think,
however, as Kant does, that it makes them any more compatible. Even
Kant's compatibalism is very qualified, since he does not conclude that
we are both determined and free, both empirical and transcendental,
but only that we can think both possibilities.

We are left, it seems to me, with the following situation: As Allison
says, on the one side, "just as we can act only under the idea of freedom, so we can think only under the idea of spontaneity."[33] That is, in
order to have empirical knowledge I must, at least implicitly, take myself
to be spontaneous, intentional and thus distinct from the sensible world
I know. In order to have empirical knowledge of myself, on the other
hand, I must take myself to be part of that sensible world and subject
to its laws.

Is Kant saying, then, that there are two selves, a transcendental and
an empirical? No, manifestly not; he is merely saying that there are two
equally necessary and incompatible descriptions that we give to ourselves. If he were making the assertion that there are two selves, then
he would be advancing a metaphysics of the subject (or subjects). But

even if Kant has not made a metaphysical assertion, he may be thought to have left us with a metaphysical question; namely, which description corresponds to the way I really am? This recalls Kant's oft-quoted statement that the critical questions of his theoretical and practical philosophy (What can I know? What should I do? What may I hope? [A805/B833]) culminate in the question of philosophical anthropology: what is man?[34] But if this is a metaphysical question, Kant does not think we can give it a metapysical—that is, theoretical—answer. A practical response is the best we can do. Here "practical" means both the "pure practical reason" of moral action, which takes freedom for granted, and the empirical "anthropology from a pragmatic standpoint," dealing with what man "as a freely acting being makes of himself, or can and should make of himself."[35]

We are now in a position to sum up our findings on the question of Kant's "metaphysics of the subject" in a way that will respond to the main concerns raised at the beginning of this chapter.

We have noted that Kant begins with the assumption that we have synthetic a priori knowledge, and, more broadly, that we have empirical knowledge, also called experience. Having stated that these are actual, he then asks how they are possible, what the conditions are of their possibility.

It cannot be stressed enough that with this starting point, as we have noted, Kant makes a radical break with the epistemological tradition of his predecessors. From Descartes through Hume, they thought it was philosophy's task to demonstrate that we have knowledge of the world—or finally, to conclude that it could not be done. Kant indeed asks whether we have knowledge of God, freedom, and immortality, but not whether we have mathematical, scientific, or, in general, experiential knowledge.

Kant asserts that experience requires not just empirical but also pure or a priori concepts, and adduces a list of such concepts—the categories. He then introduces the Transcendental Deduction, whose purpose is to demonstrate the legitimacy (or "objectivity validity") of his list by showing that "*so far as the form of thought is concerned,* through them alone does experience become possible" [daß durch sie allein Erfahrung (*der Form des Denkens nach*) möglich sei] (A93/B126, my emphasis). But the Deduction proper makes little mention of the categories in particular and seems more concerned with establishing the *Form des Denkens,* the general structure of experience into which the categories will fit. One way to explain the rewriting of the Transcendental Deduction is that the first version did not make this structure clear enough and was considerably simplified to allow its essential features to emerge. The transcendental unity of apperception, as a subjective-objective unity, *is* that structure. It is in this context that the "I think" makes its appearance.

We have seen that, in this context, Kant is far from simply asserting the existence of a transcendental subject; nor does he assert the existence of two subjects, one transcendental and one empirical. Instead, he tells us that our experience requires that we be conscious of ourselves under two incompatible descriptions; and he strongly suggests that we are not in a position to decide between them, at least theoretically, that is, metaphysically.

Of course it is the transcendental subject that is taken by many readers of Kant to be the basis of a subjective metaphysics. But we have seen that the transcendental subject is the farthest thing from being a substance for Kant. It is not a thing in the world and can certainly not be said to exist in that sense; indeed, it is not clear in what sense it can be said to exist, even though Kant says that in transcendental apperception I am conscious of my existence. We have seen that such considerations suggest that the transcendental subject does not exist at all and may be nothing but a fiction. At the very most, it seems, the transcendental subject is something that, under certain circumstances or in certain contexts, I (must?) take myself to be. Further, *what* I take myself to be in this context is not a substance with certain properties, such as thoughts or representations; in fact, if our interpretation is correct, it is precisely the substance view of the mind (the "way of ideas") that Kant seeks to avoid. What the transcendental subject relates itself to is precisely not its own properties but objects that it distinguishes from itself.

Kant's treatment of transcendental apperception places it as far away as possible from a substance/subject metaphysics in the sense of early modern philosophy. Although the synthetic unity of apperception is called the "supreme principle of all employment of the understanding" (B136), Kant insists, as we have seen, that this form of self-consciousness is not an instance of self-knowledge, or indeed of knowledge of any sort. This has always been considered one of the great puzzles of the Transcendental Deduction, and hence of the entire first Critique. It practically scandalized his contemporaries and followers. Fichte, for one, found it intolerable: how could the fundamental principle of the system of knowledge not be itself known?

When he denies that transcendental self-consciousness is self-knowledge, Kant is denying precisely what is important about Descartes' cogito, and what sustains the whole Cartesian tradition, including the empiricists. His successors, especially Fichte, thought of this as a lapsis on Kant's part, and tried to restore his philosophy to the Cartesian path. It did not occur to them that Kant knew exactly what he was doing, that he was not seeking in the self the same metaphysical *fundamentum inconcussum* sought by other modern philosophers, that he was not really a "foundationalist" in that sense at all. Yet the tendency to force Kant into the foundationalist mold has persisted among interpreters down to the present day.

Chief among these is Heidegger, who makes of Kant not only a foundationalist but an idealist whose doctrines he links, along with the rest of modern philosophy, to technology. Kant's notion of the understanding "prescribing laws to nature, and even of making nature possible" (B159f.) may seem to support perfectly the Heideggerian interpretation; but the latter overlooks completely the qualification ("as it were" [*gleichsam*]) that Kant throws in. The qualification derives from the receptivity that is part of the knowing process. If the understanding determines what counts as an object of knowledge, it does not create its objects (A92/B125), but must wait for them to be given.

The finitude of the Kantian subject is also expressed in the concept of transcendental idealism, as we have seen. The world may be more than or other than what it is under the conditions governing its appearance to us. The subject may seem, in its cognitive guise, to legislate to nature, just as, in its moral guise, it may seem to legislate to itself. But in fact both its spontaneity and its freedom can never be anything more than the necessary assumptions under which alone we can think and act. The transcendental unity of apperception is, in the cognitive sphere, the self-consciousness in which this assumption is expressed.

Thus transcendental apperception is far indeed from any kind of self-knowledge, indubitable or otherwise. We can go farther and deny even that it is a form of self-presence. As we have seen, Heidegger construes it as another instance of the metapysics of presence, which considers the subject-subject relation just another version of the subject-object relation. As such it would also fall prey to M. Frank's objection that it leads to an infinite regress and overlooks the much more intimate relation of *Vertrautheit* (familiarity or acquaintance) between consciousness and itself.

If our findings are correct, while Kant's notion of empirical self-consciousness takes the form of a special subject-object relation, transcendental apperception does not, and thus escapes the interpretations of these two critics. The special "accompanying" character of this self-consciousness, which we have compared to indirect discourse, assures us that here I relate to myself not as an object but precisely as subject of my thoughts and experiences. This suggests a kind of intimacy that leads us to classify transcendental self-consciousness, with Makkreel, as a special or "pure" feeling. It is also this character that would lead us to classify the "self" of transcendental apperception not as object in the world but as limit of the world.

But this in turn convinces us that, even though it is non-objective and non-predicative, transcendental self-consciousness brings with it, at least implicitly, a *description* of the "self of which I am conscious." According to Kant, if our interpretation is correct, it is *as* a spontaneous, thinking, intentional, and in some sense non-worldly subject that I am implicitly aware of myself in the course of experience. In fact, it is this self-awareness that makes experience possible.

THREE

Husserl

Subjectivity and Intentionality

I begin our discussion of Husserl by asking the same question I asked about Kant: does his philosophy present us with a metaphysics of the subject? As with Kant, many interpreters—not just Heidegger—would answer in the affirmative; indeed, the answer might be that if anything qualifies as a metaphysics of the subject, it is transcendental phenomenology. I want to argue against this interpretation and propose an alternative.

To do this it is necessary to return to the origins of transcendental phenomenology in the *Logical Investigations*. This in turn requires retracing the rather complicated train of thought that leads Husserl, in that work, to introduce the concept of intentionality in Investigation V. I shall trace the emergence and eventual articulation of the phenomenological method by Husserl, in order to make clear the broader context for his theory of the subject. Then we shall be in a position to understand his conception of both transcendental and empirical subjectivity.

The Emergence of Phenomenology

In volume 1, the *Prolegomena to Pure Logic*, Husserl had attacked psychologism and introduced the idea of pure logic as theory of science. When the "Investigations" proper are introduced in volume 2, the reader might expect "pure logic" actually to get under way. This does not happen. Instead, pure logic is to be subjected to "epistemological criticism and clarification" through "phenomenological investigations" (LI 248).[1] The overall title of the second volume is "Investigations on the Phenomenology and Theory of Knowledge."

The question is, what are phenomenological investigations? Husserl has introduced a new term without preparing us for it. He seems to know what it means, and in the following pages he gives us several indications of what he has in mind. But these indications do not hang together in a systematic way and appear more as a series of hints. Compared with his later intensive concern with the systematic presentation of the phenomenological method, this is quite remarkable. Husserl later claims that phenomenology made its "breakthrough" in the *Logical Investigations*. But here it is as if he had almost unwittingly stumbled on the method, practiced it with considerable success in this work, and only later realized its immense significance for philosophy. Only then, in the ensuing years, did he turn his attention to its refinement and systematic presentation as a philosophical method.

For our purposes it is important to look at what Husserl does say, in this early work, about phenomenological investigations. Phenomenology in general, he tells us, takes "experiences" (*Erlebnisse*)[2] as its focus: the phenomenology of the *Logical Investigations* will focus on a subclass of experiences: those of thinking and judging (LI 249).

With this Husserl has signaled something important and distinctive for his approach throughout: to clarify something philosophically is to relate it to direct, lived experience. Even logic, which Husserl insists is concerned like mathematics with ideal or abstract entities, relations, and truths, must be dealt with in this way. This is, one could say, the empiricist in Husserl: trace everything, no matter how abstract, back to experience. But this raises an obvious question that occurred to his readers right away: is this not a return to psychologism?

According to Husserl, the phenomenological investigations he proposes are situated in a "neutral" realm between empirical psychology and pure logic (LI 249). They must be presuppositionless, and it must be clear that they belong to the theory of knowledge, not to metaphysics (LI 265). In fact, the phenomenological theory of knowledge is not even a theory in the usual sense of the word, that is, a science that explains. Instead its aim is to shed light on or clarify (*aufklären*) and understand the knowing process (LI 265). In the first edition Husserl even called phenomenology "descriptive psychology"; later he felt that it was wrong to call it psychology at all but continued to emphasize its descriptive, as opposed to explanatory character (see LI 262).

This emphasis on the descriptive, non-explanatory character of phenomenological investigations indicates to us how they can be compatible with Husserl's attack on psychologism: to trace everything—for example, even logical entities and relations—"back to experience" might seem to be precisely the psychologistic program. But to trace something back to experience in Husserl's sense is not to explain it through experience or reduce it to experience, as empiricists often have done. In fact, one of the main points of "clarifying," Husserl tells us, is to inhibit our "by no means chance inclination to slip unwittingly from an objective to a psychological attitude" and mix up two related but distinct subject matters (LI 253). In this sense phenomenology, far from being psychologistic, will continue and consolidate the attack on psychologism.

As the Investigations proper get under way, Husserl picks up on the idea that he quotes from Mill at the beginning: we must begin with the study of language, since it is in linguistic form that "the objects which pure logic seeks to examine" (LI 250) are given. Cognition and theoretical activity issue in expressions and judgments, and these take verbal form. He begins by distinguishing the "meaningful" expressions of language from mere signs: the latter have a simple conventional or causal relation to what they signify, but no meaning as such (LI 269). Expressions have meaning. But what does it mean for an expression to have meaning? The linguistic expression by itself is merely an acoustical phenomenon (in speech) or a spatial configuration (in the case of writing). It acquires meaning thanks to a "sense-giving act" on the part of a conscious user of the language (LI 280).

Thus, Husserl's route from logic to the experience in which it is given has taken him to language and from thence to the conscious acts that are the source of its meaning. He does not tarry, then, over the phenomenon of language as such but turns instead to the notion of consciousness. With this he has arrived at his philosophical destination, or destiny: it is consciousness that will be the central focus of his attentions for the rest of his life.

It is consciousness in the sense of intentional experience, or *act*, that is the focus of Husserl's attention in Investigation 5. This is the sense that is relevant to his preoccupation with logic, and with knowledge in general. But before he gets to the discussion of intentionality he deals with consciousness in more general terms and has some important things to say about the term "experience" (*Erlebnis*) as he is using it. An experience is a subjective or conscious episode we live through: experiencing is "living through" something in this sense. Husserl wants to distinguish the awareness that belongs to this "living through" from any kind of awareness of objects. For the latter he uses the term *Erfahrung*. This is also Kant's term, and Husserl uses it in exactly the same sense: *Erfahrung* is the experience of objects in the world. In perception, for example, which is a species of *Erfahrung*, I perceive some object—for example, a tree in the garden—but I "experience" or "live through" (*ich erlebe*) the perception itself. I do not "live through" the tree, and unless I explicitly reflect, I do not perceive my perception (LI 540).

This distinction, and Husserl's terminological choice, are very important for the discussion of intentional experiences, but not all experiences are intentional. Certain kinds of sensations or feelings, for example, are related to no object: I just have them. But they are experiences in the sense that I live through them (see also LI section 14, p. 567).

Finally, Husserl turns his attention to consciousness considered as that class of experiences called "intentional," which he also terms "acts." Here Husserl draws on his teacher Franz Brentano, who used the concept of intentionality in order to distinguish between "psychic phenomena" and "physical phenomena." "Every mental phenomenon," writes Brentano, "is characterized by what the medieval schoolmen called intentional (or mental) inexistence of an object, and by what we . . . call the relation to a content, the direction to an object . . . or an immanent objectivity" (LI 554).[3] In perception something is perceived, in imagination something is imagined, in a statement something stated, in love something loved, in desire something desired, and so forth.

Husserl's purpose in introducing intentionality is not the same as Brentano's, and in fact he disagrees with Brentano on this point. As we have already noted, not all experiences are intentional, as is proved by certain kinds of feelings and sensations (LI 556). Yet as experiences they are clearly psychic or mental, indeed even conscious. Intentionality belongs only to a certain class of experiences. But this is a crucial class, not only for the clarification of logic, but for our idea of what counts as a conscious being. A being "merely having contents inside it such as the experiences of sense, but unable to interpret these objectively . . . incapable, therefore, of referring to objects" would not be a mental or conscious being, says Husserl (LI 553).

Beyond this, though, what interests Husserl is how this referring takes place, and how it does so in different ways. What exactly is the nature of this "relation to a content," "direction to an object," which is essential to this class of experiences? Husserl devotes considerable attention to answering this question. And it could be said that from his answers, all of phenomenology ultimately flows.

Husserl begins his approach to what the intentional "relation" is by saying what he thinks it is not. We might be tempted to consider it a "real relation," that is, a relation obtaining between two real things. My different ways of being conscious of some object, for example, thinking of, imagining, or seeing my friend Bill, might be construed as types of relation that obtain between Bill and me, like the relations of being taller than, or being next to. Or again, as in the tradition, as a causal relation. But the conscious acts have the feature of "taking" Bill *as* something, namely as my friend. Unlike the other relations, this one relates to Bill only under a certain description. As Husserl says, we must distinguish between the object *which* is intended and the object *as* it is intended (LI 578). Bill is undoubtedly many other things, but it is *as* my friend that I am thinking of him. Bill may not even be my friend at all (he may be a "false friend"), but it is still true that I am thinking of him and even seeing him *as* such. Furthermore, I can think of and imagine things that do not exist at all, like the god Jupiter, or even "see" things that do not exist, like the water that seems to shimmer on the road ahead on a hot day. Yet each of these experiences is still somehow, and importantly, "related to a content," "directed to an object." Here a "real relation" is clearly not to be found.

These considerations might lead us to construe intentionality as another kind of "real" relation: not between me or my consciousness and something outside, but between two things *in* consciousness. This is behind the use of the word "content," of course. The god Jupiter and the mirage do not exist outside consciousness; as we often say, they're just "in the mind." But Husserl immediately points out that this cannot be meant literally: the intentional experience of thinking of the god Jupiter "may be dismembered as one chooses in descriptive analysis, but the god Jupiter will naturally not be found in it" (558f.). This mythical entity does not exist anywhere, even in the mind. But there may be another approach, which applies also to objects that really do exist. Where the object does exist, for example, my friend Bill, we have rejected the idea of a real relation to Bill himself, and noted furthermore that we always refer to him under some description, just as we see him from some point of view. Perhaps what the mind relates to is not Bill himself but an image, picture, or representation of him. Likewise, we may have in our minds not mythical gods, but images of them.

Husserl rejects this approach as wrongheaded, devoting several pages to it (LI 593ff.).[4] But it probably deserves more. What he does not note is that this is the standard approach to knowledge in early modern philosophy, the "way of ideas" against which Kant was reacting (see chapter 2, p. 46). The conception is that what the mind relates to is not things but images of them, and the images are both caused by and similar to the things they depict. This conception is notoriously fraught with all kinds of difficulties: the skeptic will point out that we can never compare images with the things they supposedly portray; the idealist will ask how mental entities can resemble or be caused by non-mental entities; and finally, there is the danger of infinite regress: is the awareness of the mental image to be explained in turn by recourse to an image of it? And so on.

Husserl's response to what he calls this "box-within-box" [LI 557] approach to mental contents is, significantly, different from all these objections. He thinks it is simply descriptively incorrect, a simple confusion of two experiences we are quite familiar with, that is, being aware of something and being aware of an image of that thing. There are "not two things present in experience, we do not experience the object and beside it the intentional experience directed upon it . . . : only one thing is present, the intentional experience, whose essential descriptive character is the intention in question" (LI 558). The object, whether existent or non-existent, is not part of the "descriptive real make-up" of the experience (LI 559). The latter is just the intention itself, and the object is intended by it. In the case of sense perception, sensations may be part of the experience, but they should not be confused with the object: "I do not see colour-sensations but coloured things, I do not hear tone sensations but the singer's song, etc., etc." (LI 559).

These remarks reveal the manner in which the theory of consciousness as intentional actually continues and broadens the attack on psychologism. Husserl opposes the general empiricist tendency to collapse into subjective idealism or skepticism by reducing objectivity of any sort—whether in logical thinking or perception—to contents of the mind, or to confuse the two. It is necessary to distinguish the intentional experience, as directed toward some object, from the object to which it is directed. Put broadly, it is the nature of consciousness as intentionality to point beyond itself or transcend itself. Seen in this way, phenomenology makes its appearance as a kind of realism. Its aim is to clarify the nature of certain kinds of experiences, and the first thing it must do is exclude from them their objects. Indeed, at this stage "phenomenological description" was meant to focus exclusively on the subjective side (see LI 576n.). Its focus was just the *Erlebnisse*, and its purpose was to distinguish their different kinds and describe their essential structures. This Husserl called their "phenomenological content." Their "intentional content," that is, their objects, even as intended, was to be excluded (LI 576n).

The Phenomenological Method

This was the conception of "phenomenological investigations" that emerged from the *Logical Investigations* and that Husserl applied to various topics (e.g., perception of things in space, time-consciousness) in the ensuing years. His main concern was to distinguish it from psychology by insisting that its approach was not empirical but "eidetic." That is, it was not just that its aim was to describe rather than explain; what it described was not mere facts but "essences," the essential structures of experiences.

But there are certain features of this conception that inevitably led Husserl to revise it in a radical way.

Two related points emerge from my discussion so far. First, Husserl seems to want to put the experiences on one side, their objects on the other, in a neat division, and then deal exclusively with the former. But it is somehow troubling that some of the items on the object-side, like the god Jupiter, now rigorously excluded from consciousness, do not exist at all. What we have called the "realist" aspect of Husserl's approach seems to require relegating to the "real world" some things that are not real at all. If they are not part of the real world, why bother with them at all? Precisely because they form a class, indeed a very important class, of intentional objects. By excluding them from both the mind *and* the external world we have rendered them totally homeless. Somehow, they deserve better than this.

The second point is a closely related one. Phenomenology is supposed to describe experiences in essential terms; but in the case of an intentional experience, its "essential descriptive character is the intention in question" (LI 558). But the intention is *of* something, whether existent or not, outside the experience. How can one describe the experience adequately without referring to what it is of? Clearly the phenomenological description of the experience is going to have somehow to encompass its object—at the very least the object *as* it is intended. This is in fact why we cannot overlook those non-existent objects: they appear frequently as the objects of certain kinds of experiences, such as imagining, daydreaming, reading fiction, hoping, conjecturing, watching television, and possibly those where illusions and hallucinations are involved. But in the same way we cannot ignore the existent objects of such experiences as perception or judgment.

This second point leads Husserl to see that if phenomenology is really to be true to the experiences it seeks to describe, it is somehow going to have to expand its scope to include the objects of those experiences as well. The first reaction to this might be that phenomenology will thereby lose all specificity, since anything at all can be an object of consciousness. This seems to extend its scope to the whole of existence. But then how does it differ from the sciences, which together deal with the whole of existence in its various subdivisions or regions? And then phenomenology is supposed to deal with all the non-existent objects as well!

But if the project of phenomenology seems thereby to get completely out of hand, further reflection suggests that it can be at the same time brought under control and elevated to a status far more important than that originally envisaged for it.

The first point to be made has already been noted: while it is true that, in order to do justice to the intentional experience, phenomenology must treat the object of the experience, it must treat the object only as intended in that experience. Thus it would consider all possible objects of experience, but from a specific point of view.

Second, the distinction between existent and non-existent objects is one that turns up within the intentions phenomenology describes: some objects, for example, those of our fictional imagination or fantasy, are intended as not existing, while objects of perception, say, are intended as existing. But this will be true whether or not these objects actually exist independently of the intentions in question. Being intended as existing (or as not existing) has no implication at all for the actual existence of the object. Nor does the existence of the object have any implication for the nature, that is, the description, of the experience. So one can do complete justice descriptively to the experiences treated by phenomenology and drop all reference to *actual* existence—though not, of course, to intended existence.

Three things emerge so far: (1) In a certain way phenomenology has as its domain not just experiences and their intentions but also, through them, all possible objects. (2) It considers these objects always from the point of view of how they are intended only. (3) Doing so is completely indifferent to or "neutral" with regard to the actual, that is, extra-mental or extra-intentional existence of these objects. These considerations doubtless convinced Husserl that the phenomenological approach he had "stumbled on" in the *Logical Investigations* had the status of a genuine philosophical discipline, combining a universal scope with a specific methodological point of view.

But one further consideration, which we have not mentioned so far, was even more important. Implicit in everything Husserl does in the *Logical Investigations,* but never thematized, is the first-person point of view.

In a way this should be obvious. Phenomenology's initial concern was with *Erlebnisse,* with the subjective rather than the objective. Yet

Husserl's first reflections on the phenomenological method seem to point away from the first-person character of his approach, as if to take a distance from it. The idea of phenomenology an as "eidetic" discipline, dealing descriptively with the essences of certain kinds of experience, suggests that it applies to any and all such experiences, not just mine. Objects too, of course, are treated in essential terms.

Nevertheless, the idea behind the shift to phenomenological investigations, that the philosophical "clarification" of anything requires showing how it relates back to the *Erlebnis*, or lived experience, has further implications. The nature of such experiences, as we saw, is that to have them is to have a kind of intimate, pre-objective awareness of them. Even the meaning of language derives from the language-user's act (that is, intentional experience) of bestowing meaning. And to "perform" such an act is to be directly aware that you do so.[5] Indeed, it seems that the only way of having such direct access to such an experience is to *have* it, the only way of knowing such an act is to *perform* it. Thus presumably the way to begin talking about experiences in a philosophical way is to consult one's own experience (to reflect).

And so it happens that when Husserl enters his mature "middle" period, ready to introduce phenomenology as a full-fledged method for philosophy, he introduces it literally and quite explicitly in the voice of the first person. In the 1913 *Ideas* 1, when he presents what he calls the fundamental phenomenological outlook—after the preliminaries are out of the way—he writes: "We begin our considerations as human beings who are living... '*in the natural attitude.*' What this signifies we shall make clear in simple meditations which can best be carried out in the first person singular" (ID1 51). Then: "I am conscious of a world ...," and so on. And while he occasionally reverts to the authorial "we," addressing his readers, (e.g., "For us, who are striving toward the entrance-gate of phenomenology" [ID1 56]), it is clear from here on out that phenomenology is actually being "done" only when the first-person singular is being used.

The great significance of this adoption of the first person is acknowledged by Husserl, not only by introducing it explicitly in the text, as we have noted, but also by a historical gesture: he invokes the philosopher most often associated with the first-person approach, Descartes, first indirectly, by employing the term "meditations," and then directly by several explicit references to that author. He also employs the term "cogito" in a crucial role. Thus begins a long association that reaches its high point in the *Cartesian Meditations* of 1929. Though Husserl is always critical of Descartes on many points, and even has occasion to criticize his own use of the "Cartesian approach" as misleading (see CR 155) and to supplement it with other ways to the "entrance-gate" of phenomenology,[6] his deep kinship with Descartes is never denied, and never absent.

We have already pointed out that the first-person approach, like many other features of the full-fledged phenomenological method, is already implicit in the phenomenology of the *Logical Investigations*. Even there, as phenomenologist, one would seem to be dependent first and foremost on the reflective consultation of one's own experience. We noted Husserl's emphasis on dealing with "essences" and the apparent discrepancy between that and the first-person approach. But it should be pointed out that the combination of these two elements is not new; in fact, it is already found precisely in Descartes. The style of first-person meditation, which includes even autobiographical, narrative elements in both the *Discourse on Method* and the *Meditations* of Descartes, should not mislead us into thinking that the point of these writings is to inform us about the personal life of their author. This may be the major point of the most famous forerunner of Husserl and Descartes in this genre, Augustine in his *Confessions*. It is not the only point there, of course, but the author's life and his experience of conversion, in all their particularity, are meant to serve as a model for others. Descartes speaks of himself and his own thoughts, but his readers are supposed to recognize that what he says is true of their own thoughts too, not just by coincidence but in virtue of being true of any and all thoughts, that is, of being universally true. This is obviously the point of Husserl's first-person meditations as well. In *Ideas* 1, he is adamant that phenomenology remains a "science of essences."

But there are very important ways in which Husserl is taken beyond the phenonenology of the *Logical Investigations,* once he has openly confessed, as it were, to the first-person approach. He is no longer just speaking of experiences of different types—perception and perceptual judgment, say, or memory versus imagination—and classifying them and contrasting the different ways in which they relate to their objects. He is also looking at them with respect to how they fit into *my* mental life as a whole. And after expanding phenomenology to include the objects of experience as experienced, he now looks at them not just as they are intended in this or that experience, but also as they relate to each other in the context of *my* experience as a whole.

Two consequences flow immediately from this consideration, which were totally lacking in *Logical Investigations*. The first is that, on the side of experiences, they must be seen in their mulitiplicity as a temporal flow, and some attention must be paid to how their unity as *my* experiences is to be described. Husserl had of course taken up the subject of "internal time-consciousness" in lectures, notably in 1905. It is clear in this early treatment that the mature stage of the phenomenological method had not yet been reached. In *Ideas* 1 Husserl mentions the crucial importance of the temporal dimension of consciousness, even though he postpones its detailed treatment (ID1 193f.); but he does pay a great deal of attention to the topic of unity in devoting attention to the concept of the pure Ego—a concept he had explicitly rejected in the *Logical Investigations.*

On the objective side, Husserl speaks now not merely of objects, but of "my surrounding world" (*meine Umwelt*) and the "world [*Welt*] of the natural attitude." Objects of perception are described as experienced in their spatiotemporal context, as standing out against an indistinct and receding background, and as endowed with uses, values, and names. Animals and persons are mentioned as belonging to the experienced world as well. Mathematical and other ideal "worlds" are discussed with reference to how they relate to the spatiotemporal world when we think of and refer to them. Once Husserl has moved to speaking about the world, it becomes clear that his phenomenology is not just about experiences, or even about experiences and their objects, but about the first-person standpoint itself. We could say it is about what it means to be conscious or to be a conscious being, to be a subject, a self, or an ego.

Now all the elements I have discussed so far come together in Husserl's introduction of the phenomenological method as such. It is not just objects I am conscious of, but with them, implicitly, the whole world. To describe my experience phenomenologically, then, means describing the whole world of objects, and possible objects, of my experience. The universality of phenomenology's scope thus becomes clear. Yet, just as its task is to describe not objects *which*, but objects *as* they are intended, so the world becomes a theme just *as*—that is, with respect to *how*—it figures in my experience. The world, Husserl says, is the correlate of the "natural attitude" underlying all ordinary experience. The "thesis" of this attitude is as follows: " 'The' world is always there as an actuality . . . is always factually existent" (ID1 57).

But now one further consideration, already discussed, becomes a keystone of the method: just as my consciousness of an object *as existing* does not imply its actual existence, so my "natural attitude" toward the world as existing does not imply the world's actual existence either. This means that when phenomenology's task is to describe my experience and the world as experienced, it is in no way committed to the extra-mental or extra-intentional existence of the world and is free to drop all reference to or claim about that existence. Husserl proposes that we do just that, that is, "suspend" the thesis of the natural attitude itself, "bracket" or "switch off" (*ausschalten*) everything the thesis encompasses with respect to being (ID1 61). It is here, of course, that Descartes gets mentioned: Husserl recognizes that what he proposes bears some resemblence to that philosopher's doubting procedure. But he insists he is neither negating the world's existence nor even doubting it, he is simply suspending it. This he calls the phenomenological epoche. We are perfectly free, he says, to do this at any time (ID1 58).

To which the obvious response is, Perhaps so, but why *should* we do it? What is to be gained by this curious manoeuver?

Why Bracket?

Husserl actually has different ways of responding to this question, and it is useful to consider them and distinguish them from one another.

In *Ideas* 1, immediately after proposing the phenomenological epoche, Husserl raises the question of what is to be gained by it. Is the point to establish a new eidetic discipline, say an eidetic psychology, a science of essences rather than one of facts? No, he says; our goal is *"the acquisition of a new region of being never before delimited in its own peculiarity"* (ID1 63; cf. CM 27). Husserl uses the notion of regions of being throughout his work during this period, without considering it problematic. The region of physical reality or spatiotemporal being, which is addressed by the physical sciences, is always the paradigm case. But by considering it one region among others, Husserl indicates that he rejects any form of physicalistic reductionism and places this region alongside other regions of being, namely, those addressed by the psychological and the human sciences. The second volume of the *Ideas*, "Studies in the Phenomenology of Constitution," is broken down according to just these regions, "material nature," "animal nature," and "the spiritual world" [*die geistige Welt*].[7]

Now Husserl seems to be saying that another region of being, which he will call the region of pure consciousness (see ID1 105ff.), has been there all along, but unnoticed, alongside the other regions. This region can now be discerned and, thanks to the new method, explored in full by a new science exclusively devoted to this task. This would presumably be justification enough for the phenomenological epoche: it opens up a new terrain, affording access to something not previously known or seen.

An obvious question suggests itself: if the new region is that of consciousness, how does it differ from the region already well known, that of the mind or psyche, which is dealt with by psychology? Husserl devotes much attention to answering this question, since he is especially concerned that phenomenology not be confused with psychology of any kind. Psychology treats consciousness in its natural setting, so to speak; that is, it considers it as belonging to real persons in the world, as being related causally through their bodies to the world around them, and so on. In other words, its object is empirical consciousness, and it treats this object in the manner of an empirical science, explaining facts and events rather than describing essences. The object of phenomenology is "pure" consciousness in the sense that all reference to its empirical setting is dropped—or rather bracketed.

What is more, since phenomenology extends to the objects of consciousness as intended, its scope is broader than that of psychology. In fact, if anything genuinely qualifies as a "new" and unexplored region, it is this: objects, indeed the whole world of objects for a consciousness, treated strictly as they are intended by consciousness. Here is something no one previously thought to address systematically as a domain for scientific treatment. And of course it is not as if consciousness and its objects made up two separate domains; they belong strictly together as the two sides of the complex structure of intentionality. Consciousness purely as intending a world and the world purely as intended by consciousness indeed make up a unified domain that is distinguishable from any of the domains previously mentioned as regions of being, such as the region of physical reality or the region of psychic reality considered by themselves.

However, this explanation and justification of the phenomenological epoche—that it opens up and explores a new region of being—is not enough to express Husserl's reasons for proposing it. He obviously thinks of phenomenology as more than merely a new regional ontology alongside the others. Its region of being must be somehow privileged in relation to the others. The region of pure consciousness must be considered, as he says, the "primal region" (*Urregion*), the "primal category of all being." It is the realm of "absolute" being to which all other regions of being "are relative and on which they are therefore all essentially dependent" (ID1 171).

The privilege thus accorded the region of pure consciousness needs to be further explained, for it lends itself to a very problematic interpretation—an interpretation that often seems to be supported, it must be said, by Husserl's own words. The above formulation seems to suggest that the other regions are somehow contained in the region of consciousness, which would mean, in effect, that physical reality, for example, is contained within consciousness. But this can hardly be what

Husserl has in mind, since he has argued from the start against the idea that the object of consciousness—including, of course, but not limited to physical objects—is really contained (*reell enthalten*) in consciousness itself. This would be the psychologistic position he has opposed since the *Logical Investigations*. In fact, he scrupulously avoids the language of containedness. The "most radical of all ontological distinctions," he says, is that between "being *as consciousness* and being as something which becomes '*manifested*' in consciousness, 'transcendent' being" (ID1 171). "This '*transcendence*' is part of the intrinsic sense of anything wordly," he writes in the *Cartesian Meditations*: "[N]either the world nor any worldly Object is a piece of my Ego, to be found in my conscious life as a really inherent part of it" (CM 26).

What then could it mean to say that the other regions are "relative to" and even "dependent on" the region of pure consciousness? Husserl could hardly mean that physical reality, while transcending consciousness, depends for its being on consciousness, that consciousness somehow brings it into or sustains it in being, or that without consciousness it would not exist. Husserl has declined to speak of any causal relationship between consciousness and its objects, and the whole possibility of the epoche depends precisely on the claim that consciousness and its objects are ontologically independent of each other. If the epoche is in effect, all reference to the being of transcendent reality has in any case been dropped.

What then is relative to or dependent on consciousness? Not the being of transcendent reality, but merely its *sense* of being, including precisely its "intrinsic sense" of being transcendent. The theory of regions of being belongs to what Husserl calls ontology. It considers the different possible modes of being, develops the "material a priori" distinctions between being a physical entity, say, and being a mental or cultural entity, and so forth. It also includes the *formal* a priori theory of what applies to all entities just as entities. All formal logic and mathematics would belong here. But now Husserl has shifted from ontology to phenomenology, again tracing the regions of being back to their "source" in experience. From the phenomenological, as opposed to the ontological point of view, all regions of being are regions of possible objects for consciousness, and it is in their capacity as objects, rather than simply as entities, that they are considered. From this point of view beings and even regions of being are indeed, even trivially, relative to or dependent on consciousness. To be an object is to be an object *for* consciousness, to have meaning is to have meaning *for* a meaning-bestowing intentional act.

Thus if the phenomenological epoche is justified because of the "new region of being" it opens up, it is not because this region swallows up all the others, but because it deals with the source of the meaning of all the others, including even their meaning of being transcendent. According to Husserl, consciousness, subjectivity, the ego, and so forth—that is, all the major themes of phenomenology—acquire the name "transcendental" just because of their relation to the transcendence of the world. Indeed, that is why phenomenology itself acquires the name "transcendental" (CM 26; cf. ID1 209).

There is another justification for the epoche that runs through the Ideas, and plays an even more prominent role in the *Cartesian Meditations*—perhaps because it is a particularly Cartesian motif. This is the idea that by turning back reflectively to my own experiences, and refraining from all claims about the existence of the world, I limit myself to a domain I can know with absolute certainty. The tree I see may be other than I take it to be, or may not exist at all; but that I seem to see it, and that it seems such and such to me, is certain and indubitable (Cf. especially §§ 44–46 of ID1, § 7 of CM). It is to be noted that this realm of indubitable evidence includes not only consciousness but also its objects, provided one restricts oneself to describing them *as* experienced—*cogitata qua cogitata*, as Husserl calls them in *Cartesian Meditations* (CM 39).

Thus the epoche seems to make possible a science whose claims are based on a kind of certainty found in none of the other sciences. Only such a science, Husserl seems to think, would genuinely qualify as philosophy. And because it takes in the whole world, in the special sense I have described, it would be universal in scope as well.

There are a couple of problems with this justification for the epoche, however, especially if we give it too Cartesian an interpretation. The first is that Husserl seems to back off from his claim of certainty for phenomenology. In *Ideas* 1 Husserl insists that transcendent reality is always given one-sidedly or inadequately, while immanent reality (i.e., my own experiences) is always given adequately (ID1 95). Even there he qualifies this when he considers the temporal character of experience (ID1 97). By the time he writes *Cartesian Meditations*, he tries to deal with this problem by distinguishing between adequate and apodictic evidence. He now admits that reflection does not provide adequate evidence, given the elusive and flowing character of conscious life; but he insists that there is a core of apodictic evidence to the Cartesian cogito. When pressed to say how far it extends, however, Husserl mentions only *"ego sum* or *sum cogitans,"* which provides us with "a first apodictically existing basis to stand on" (CM 22). But that, it must be said, is precious little. He does say later, without attempting to justify it, that there is "a *universal apodictically experienceable structure* of the Ego (for example, the immanent temporal form belonging to the stream of subjective processes)" (CM 28). Thus, in addition to knowing that I exist I know something about my essence. Anything beyond that, it seems, can claim neither adequacy nor apodicticity.

The second problem concerns the relation of the new, apodictically based science to the other sciences already in existence—what Husserl calls the sciences of the natural attitude. Descartes thought that by withdrawing to the realm of the cogito he could find a foundation for all the other sciences, justifying his previously naive belief in the external world. Husserl criticizes him for thinking that with the cogito he had grasped a "tag-end of the world," the *substantia cogitans*, from which he could causally infer the existence of the rest of the world (CM 24). For Husserl no such inference is possible, the existence of the world is not in question, and if phenomenology is to have a bearing on the other sciences, it will not be the sort envisaged by Descartes.

Yet obviously Husserl thinks it does have a bearing. In place of Descartes' foundationalism he proposes "the idea of a transcendental grounding of knowledge" (CM 27). Such a grounding is in accord with what we have already said about the relation between the "region of pure consciousness" and the other regions of being. The latter are neither swallowed up by the former nor do they simply stand alongside it as part of the world. Instead, phenomenology explores the manner in which they "transcend" consciousness by virtue of the meaning it bestows upon them.

Thus we return again to the theme of transcendence and to Husserl's idea of phenomenology as transcendental philosophy. Following Kant in using this terminology, Husserl even refers to phenomenology as transcendental idealism (CM 83). But it is important to note that what we called the original *realism* of phenomenology is never abandoned. That is, no attempt is made to reduce or absorb the object of intentionality into consciousness. For this reason, using the term "reduction" in place of "epoche" is very misleading. On the contrary, the *transcendence* of object and world, which is precisely their *non*-reducibility (to consciousness), is taken seriously and subjected to careful analysis. On the other hand, the point is not to deduce or infer the world's existence—much less to explain it or indeed explain consciousness—but to clarify and describe the sense of that existence as it is manifested in consciousness.

But the realism of phenomenology's opening move does not remain naive; it is not content simply to assert the transcendence of the world, but wants to know what it means to assert it or believe it. As we have seen, phenomenology is called "transcendental" because of its focus on the problem of transcendence—as Kant would say, on the conditions for its possibility.

These considerations now permit us to give another answer—and in some ways a surprising one—to the question I have been addressing in this section: *why* perform the epoche, *why* suspend the thesis of the natural attitude? The natural attitude is Husserl's name for the naive and unreflected belief in the transcendence of the world. We suspend it not in order to go off into some hitherto undiscovered region of being, nor in order to secure premises from which we can deduce its truth, nor in order somehow to deny its truth. Rather, we suspend its validity, the better to understand the natural attitude itself. *As* naive and unreflected, the natural attitude lies deep and is hidden from consciousness itself. In later works Husserl calls it *Urglaube* or primal belief, and he describes it as the world-life of consciousness, whose always pre-given horizon is the life-world. It has such a hold on consciousness that we must draw back from it, in order to recognize even that it is there.

Thus, the relationship between the phenomenological and the natural attitudes is a peculiarly intimate one. Even though the phenomenological method involves precisely the suspension of the natural attitude, the natural attitude is never really left behind. There are two senses in which this is so. First, if the purpose of the reduction is to understand the natural attitude, then the latter is in a sense the source of all its descriptions. All the sciences, including the *Geisteswissenschaften*, are based on the natural attitude, or as Husserl says later, arise on the basis of the pre-given life-world. A phenomenological clarification of the sciences involves understanding how the undifferentiated natural standpoint gets narrowed into the "naturalistic" attitude of the natural sciences, on the one hand, and the "personalistic" attitude of the human sciences, on the other (cf. ID2 183). Clearly such understanding is not possible unless the phenomenologist continues in some sense to live in the natural attitude that is being described. Presumably because it is impossible to live in the natural attitude and to observe it phenomenologically at the same time, Husserl often characterizes the pattern of investigation as a zigzag.

Continuing to live in the natural attitude is not something we need great effort to do. It is, after all, natural to us, and it is the suspension that requires the effort. This is the second sense in which the natural attitude is never really left behind in phenomenology. Husserl repeatedly warns us against falling back into it, as if it exerted a kind of gravitational pull against which we had constantly to struggle. It is rather the phenomenological approach that goes against the grain, as Husserl already remarked in the *Logical Investigations* (LI 254). In *Ideas* 2, Husserl even goes so far as to call it "artificial" (ID2 189). Thus, phenomenology cannot forget its origins in the natural attitude, nor should it. In phenomenology consciousness turns back on itself; what it finds, and attempts to describe and explain, is a consciousness immersed naively in the world. Phenomenology is thus forever poised on the line between the natural and the transcendental standpoints.

Transcendental and Empirical Subjectivity

We are now in a position to return to the question with which we began: does Husserl's phenomenology present us with a metaphysics of the subject? Let us recall some of the things we have established about Husserl's enterprise.

We have seen that phenomenology is not just the eidetic description and classification of experiences, but is about the first-person standpoint as a whole, that is, what it means to have experiences, what it means to be a self or subject or ego. It is further about the world of objects, not in general, but in relation to such a subject. It suspends the "thesis" of the natural attitude, not in order to leave this attitude behind or go off into some other domain, but in order to understand better the natural attitude itself. Rather than simply living naively in the natural attitude, as we did before, and as we still do most of the time, we reflect on it, on the consciousness that makes it up, and on the meaning of the objects and the world of the natural attitude. Insofar as this world has for consciousness the sense of transcendence, consciousness and the subject of consciousness are designated "transcendental." Thus it can be said that the central focus of phenomenology is the transcendental subject or ego.

The question of whether phenomenology is a metaphysics of the subject will obviously turn on the status of this transcendental subject, and on whether phenomenology's treatment of it can be called metaphysical.

It is to be noted that the subject considered in this sense is very much a function of Husserl's method. While the term "transcendental subject" reminds us of Kant, it is important for now to restrict ourselves to Husserl's own sense of it. It would seem that the Husserlian transcendental subject cannot emerge or make any sense at all apart from the phenomenological epoche or reduction. As Husserl says, "[A]s an Ego in the natural attitude, I am likewise and at all times a transcendental Ego, but . . . I know about this only by executing phenomenological reduction" (CM 37). This subject comes to light when we begin to reflect on it; but it must be emphasized that the reflection required is of a special sort. It is precisely "transcendental" and not "natural" reflection, as Husserl tells us in *Cartesian Meditations* (CM 33).

Reflection, of course, is not peculiar to phenomenology, or even to philosophy. I reflect whenever I turn my attention away from the world and other persons and direct it back toward myself and my thoughts and experiences. This is an everyday procedure and may serve many purposes: clarification and criticism of my thoughts, for example, or revision, rejection or correction of my plans and projects, and so on. Reflection in this sense has also served as the basis of the notion of psychological introspection, and as the source of the "first-person perspective" of much modern philosophy descended from Descartes. In any case the self becomes object to itself, consciousness is aware of consciousness.

But such reflection remains thoroughly within the natural attitude. What this means is that "we stand on the footing of the world already given as existing" (CM 34). I remain committed to the existence of the world—the thesis of the natural attitude is still in force—and simply take myself and my consciousness to be among its constituents. It is very different to suspend that thesis, as indicated by the phenomenological method; for when I do that, the entire world acquires the status "as intended" or "as meant" by me in my conscious life. Its transcendence is now just its *meaning* for me, and my consciousness is *transcendental* since it is being considered as the source of that meaning. Phenomenological reflection is thus transcendental reflection in virtue of the way the *transcendence* of the world is treated; it is not simply given or taken for granted, but suspended in order to be thematized or reflected upon.

From these two forms of reflection, of course, two very different conceptions of the subject emerge. Thus we encounter in Husserl something very much like the distinction we have dealt with in Kant between the empirical and the transcendental subject. Any assessment of Husserl regarding a possible "metaphysics of the subject" will have to be clear on this distinction. As with Kant, we may best approach it by speaking of each conception of the subject in terms of the consciousness we have of it. As before, we can speak of "the self of which

I am conscious" and the "consciousness of self," and distinguish under each of these headings the empirical from the transcendental. We have already made a start by linking the two concepts of subject with natural and transcendental reflection. These are two forms of the "consciousness of self" I shall have to elaborate on. Before I do that, however, let us look at what Husserl has to say about the distinction between the two subjects themselves.

The Self of Which I Am Conscious

In *Ideas* 2, which is devoted to "studies in the phenomenology of constitution," there is a long discussion of the "pure (transcendental) Ego" and how it differs from the "empirical Ego." The latter is also called the "empirical subject," the "soul," the "real psychic Ego," and "I as man" or human being—"*Ich-Mensch*" (ID2 98–99). In asking after the constitution of something, Husserl is interested in how such a thing is given in experience, and in the subjective and objective context of its givenness.

In the case of the empirical subject, Husserl is initially interested in the object of the science of psychology, and he wants to trace this object (as is usual in phenomenology) back to its appearance in ordinary experience. He describes the empirical subject as a "substantial reality," by which he means that "the soul is, in a sense similar to that of the material Body-thing, a substantial-real unity, versus the pure Ego, which, according to our exposition, is not such a unity" (ID2 128). Husserl lays a good deal of stress on the analogy between the "thing" and the "soul," even though he acknowledges that the soul is not a spatial entity and that it has entirely different sorts of properties—for example, talents, emotions, intellectual capacities, character, and so on. The analogy holds because of the relation between the psychic subject's properties and behavior (*Zustände*), on the one hand, and its "circumstances" or surroundings (*Umstände*), on the other. "The soul (or psychic subject) behaves as it does under the pertinent circumstances and in a regulated way" (ID2 132). In other words, like the physical thing, the empirical ego stands in relations of regular causal dependency with the things and events that happen around it.

The closest and most intimate thing to which it relates in this way is, of course, its own body. And through the body it relates to the rest of the physical world. But its relations to the body are not those of one "thing" to another: the soul is not a thing and the body is the "lived" or "living" body (*Leib*) rather than mere *Körper* (ID2 143). Husserl devotes much attention to the "aesthetic" and "kinesthetic" body and its role in perception (cf. ID2 6off.). He warns that the soul-body dependencies he describes here are not to be assimilated to material causality (ID2 140). And in any case, the empirical subject in question here is not the soul as distinct from the body, but "the *concrete unity* of Body and soul, human (or animal) subject" (ID2 146).

The empirical ego's "circumstances" are not only physical. Unlike the thing, the psyche is endowed with memory and hence has a relation of dependency to its own previous states (ID2 140). And finally, its relations with its surroundings are *intersubjective* and hence *social* relations.

Once he has reached this level, Husserl is aware that he is speaking of the human subject not so much in psychological as in "humanistic" terms; that is, in a frame of reference that corresponds more to the "humanities" (*Geisteswissenschaften*) than to psychological—and especially psychophysical—research. Here the term "Geist" is more important than "Seele," and the term "person" is introduced as well. Here the subject's relations to its surroundings are described as those of the ego to its "surrounding world" [*Umwelt*] (ID2 149f). I "react" to the things around me in a way that cannot be described merely in causal terms or even in those of regularity between states and circumstances. When I act and behave in certain ways toward things and other persons around me, "I feel myself conditioned" by them, "though this obviously does not mean psychophysically conditioned." Instead I react to the meaning they have in my experience.

In short, the personal subject is at least in part an intentional subject and its relations to its surroundings are intentional relations (see ID2 226f). If it is still proper to speak of an interaction, of actions, behaviors, and experiences being "caused" by things, this is no longer physical causality but "motivational causality" (ID2 227). The concept of motivation, discussed in detail by Husserl, is that of the "fundamental lawfulness of spiritual life" (ID2 231). There are rational and esthetic motivations, empathetic and emotional motivations, often occasioned by envisioned or imagined objects or situations that do not even exist. Obviously these are not causal relations. At the same time they are thoroughly intertwined with real causal relations between me and my surroundings.

Thus it is by no means the case that in natural reflection I am aware of myself merely as a thing in causal interaction with the physical world. Intentionality and subjectivity enter in here too, and my surroundings can be described as a tissue of meanings. Indeed, in the natural attitude it can be said that this "spiritual" or "personalistic" sense predominates. It is this aspect of the natural attitude that is refined and thematized in the various humanistic disciplines. These deal not only with human beings as subjects of thought, action, artistic creation, and so on, but also with the *human world* of artifacts, works of art and literature, social and legal institutions, scientific theories, and so on, all of which are what they are only in virtue of subjective, intentional acts.

Clearly the concept of the subject that emerges in this discussion bears many resemblances to that of the transcendental subject, and yet we are still presumably "on the footing" of the natural attitude. Though Husserl does not say this very clearly, the "naturalistic" and the "personalistic" attitudes distinguished in *Ideas* 2 are obviously both included in the "natural attiude" of *Ideas* 1. Here Husserl is interested in how the world of the natural attitude contains within itself the entities and relations that can become the objects of the natural sciences, the humanities, and, somehow between the two, scientific psychology. This happens thanks to the predominance of one "attitude," "apprehension," or "apperception" over another. When this occurs, it is not that we focus our attention on one type of object to the exclusion of others—persons versus things, for example—but that we look at the whole world under one aspect rather than another. Human beings can be seen as physical objects, animals, or persons; things—even natural things—can be looked at as mere physical objects or as useful, valuable, pleasing, and so on, in the human world of persons and communities.

What Husserl does not stress clearly enough at this stage is the unity of the natural attitude and its world prior to and independently of their division into these specialized realms of concern. It was this problem that gave rise to the concept of the *life-world* in his last work, *The Crisis of European Sciences*. In *Ideas* 1 and 2 Husserl is still primarily a philosopher of science—or rather, of the sciences, concerned with clarifying the distinctions between the physical, psychological, and human sciences. In *Crisis* he recognizes that understanding the sciences means understanding the unity out of which they emerge. Further, he recognizes that engaging in science is not the only human activity—that in fact it has emerged relatively late in human history—and that he must address the problem of the world at the pre-scientific level not just as in relation to the sciences but as a phenomenological theme in its own right (cf. CR 132).

From the point of view of the differences between the sciences—that is, the large differences between physics, psychology, and the humanities—the natural attitude and its world, the pre-or extra-scientific life-world, may seem a curious and even incoherent amalgam of different conceptual schemes: body, soul, causality, motivation, intentionality, and so on. Indeed, it may well be this incoherence that leads us to employ radically different concepts for dealing with it scientifically. But in everyday life, independently of the scientific concern for coherence, it has an integrated character that we take for granted without question. Things are both physical objects and items of value, use, and enjoyment. Persons are at once bodies interacting causally and subjects relating motivationally and intentionally with their surroundings.

Thus when we return to our question of how the "empirical" subject appears in "natural reflection," on the footing of the natural attitude, we must come to the following conclusions: I appear to myself as a subject within a world to which I relate in causal-bodily ways and intentional-motivational ways. The things and persons around me literally push, pull, and jostle me, but they also "move" me emotionally, attract my attention, inspire my thought and action (which in turn affect them causally). These latter, non-physical interactions are possible only in virtue of meanings that I bestow upon the things and persons around me.

But the fact remains that I also take the things and persons around me to exist independently of the meanings I bestow upon them, and to interact in ways that are totally heedless of my mental or intentional life; and I take myself, with all my mental life, to exist *within* and *among* these things and persons. In other words, within the natural attitude, while the ways of my interaction with the world around me are many, some causal, some intentional, my essential relation to the world is that of a part to a whole; and the other parts of this whole would still exist if I were not here and would, except for a few small details, be essentially unchanged. All this is implied by the fact that I am reflecting "on the footing" of the natural attitude.

What happens, now, when I deny myself that footing by performing the phenomenological reduction? In particular, what sort of subject emerges when my reflection is no longer natural, but rather transcendental?

Many of Husserl's remarks on the transcendental ego, from *Ideas* 1 and 2 through *Cartesian Meditations* and other texts, have to do with the unity of consciousness running through the flowing, temporal multiplicity of its experiences. In *Ideas* 1 he calls it a "transcendence in immanence" (ID1 133) to suggest that this unity, given in and through all experiences, nevertheless transcends them. As he elaborates on this idea the "pure ego" becomes increasingly concrete: it is by no means a purely "thinking" or rational subject; it is also immersed in the emotional life, it is passive as well as active, it is practical as well as theoretical (see ID2 103–107). In short, it is the subject of the entire range of conscious life. In *Cartesian Meditations* Husserl distinguishes broadly between the ego's role as identical pole of experiences and as "substrate of habitualities," that is, as acquiring convictions, "abiding style," even "personal character" (CM 66–67). Are these not precisely the characteristics of the "empirical ego"?

What is perhaps even more remarkable is that for Husserl this ego, understood as unity in multiplicity, is itself constituted in consciousness (ID2 109, 119f.). The term "constitution" is usually used by Husserl in relation to objects, indeed transcendent objects, that is, worldly things whose sense is to exist independently of consciousness. In perception, for example, the object is "constituted" as a unity for consciousness through a multiplicity of appearances. As Husserl says in *Cartesian Meditations* (CM 39), the primary function of consciousness is "synthesis," the joining together of disparate elements to effect the unity of an appearing object. But consciousness is itself a multiplicity of temporally flowing experiences, and Husserl's idea is that this multiplicity is unified from within through an internal time-consciousness. The "pure ego" is just the name for this unity, which can thus be said to be "constituted" by internal time-consciousness itself (ID2 109).

But we should not be led by these features of the pure ego into thinking that it is indistinguishable from the empirical ego. In speaking of the ego as pole of unity and as substrate of habitualities, Husserl is simply attempting a phenomenological description of certain features of consciousness. If the ego in these senses is constituted, it is still not "transcendent" in the sense that it belongs to the world. In fact, both senses are absorbed into what Husserl calls the "full concreteness" of the ego (CM 67), which is said to be not constituted but self-constituted. But this full concreteness also includes the world as intended (i.e., as transcendence), which is constituted in and through the self-constituting ego. As if himself confused by this apparent proliferation of egos, even at the transcendental level, Husserl in the *Crisis* increasingly opts for the term "transcendental subjectivity" to describe the full range of conscious life from the transcendental standpoint.

The key to the difference between transcendental and empirical subjects is to be found not in the internal structures of consciousness— that is, in its relation to itself—but rather in its relation to the world. Since the epoche abstains from asserting the independent existence of worldly things, all that is left is the world *as intended* by consciousness. As given in natural reflection the empirical ego or *Ich-Mensch* relates in both intentional and real-causal ways to the world, but in any case, as we saw, as part to whole. As given in transcendental reflection, by contrast, the pure or transcendental ego relates purely and exclusively

intentionally to the world, not as part to whole but as subject to object—or rather, as subject to horizon of objects.

For the world, as Husserl stresses in the *Crisis* (CR 143), is not itself
an object but the universal horizon or background of all possible objects. To be an object for consciousness is to stand within the world,
which in this broadest sense serves as background even for those non-
existent and those ideal objects that do not belong to the world of
spatiotemporal reality. Indeed, we can say that the condition for being
an object is to stand in precisely that part-whole relation to the world
we have just been speaking about. If this is so, then the subject that
appears in transcendental reflection is not an object at all, but rather,
as the subject of intentionality, it is that which makes objects possible
as objects, that is, as given to consciousness. In exactly the same way the
transcendental subject is what makes the world possible *as world*, that
is, as horizon of objects for a subject.

To summarize: I have been discussing Husserl's version of the difference between empirical and transcendental subjectivity. Taking my
cue from his distinction between natural and transcendental reflection,
I have tried to describe "the self of which I am conscious" when I
reflect in these ways. What has emerged is that the distinction can best
be formulated not so much by speaking of the "two egos" themselves
as by determining how they stand in relation to the world. Let us draw
together what we have found.

First, the *empirical subject*. Here the self is apprehended as relating in
both causal and intentional ways to other things. But it is above all
within the world, situated among the independently existing things of the
world. As such, it can be characterized as an object for reflection, a
"subject" in the metaphysical sense of substance, of certain properties
and kinds of properties ("states") that distinguish it as a thing from
other things within the world.

The *transcendental subject*, by contrast, is characterized exclusively in
terms of intentionality. Thus its relation to things and states of affairs
in the world is a meaning-giving relation, which is independent of
the existence of those things. But this is also true of its relation to the
world as a whole. Thus the transcendental subject is not within the
world at all, but is, as Husserl says in the *Crisis* (CR 178) exclusively
subject *for* the world. Since it is not within the world, it is not an object
at all in any usual sense, that is, something that is given to consciousness against the background of the world. Rather than being an object
it is the "condition of the possibility" of there being objects at all, and
indeed, of there being a world. That is, as subject of its own inten-

tionality, this subject can be seen as the *source*, not, of course, of the existence of the world or the things in it, but of their *meaning*, and indeed their status *as* objects and *as* world for a subject.

The Consciousness of Self

These two conceptions of self or subject, as we have seen, correspond to two forms of reflection, which can likewise be designated empirical and transcendental. These are the two forms of "the consciousness of self" we must now examine more closely.

Empirical or "natural" reflection arises in the course of life, as we noted, and can be practical as well as theoretical. That is, it can serve to clarify and focus my activities, or it can become the basis of a contemplation or observation of myself as an object of knowledge. In either case it never leaves the natural attitude behind, and it is in this respect like the consciousness of every other worldly object, including other persons. I may have a different sort of access, and indeed a more direct and intimate access, to my own thoughts and feelings, than in the awareness I have of others, but I am for myself, in this kind of reflection, just another object or entity within the world. This means that not only the self, but the world itself is posited.

In transcendental reflection, on the other hand, in which the transcendental subject appears, the situation is very different: while I am presumably aware of myself as existing, the world's existence is bracketed and the world figures only as the horizon of all possible intended objects. The transcendental subject emerges through transcendental reflection as the unity of the intentional consciousness through which objects and world are so intended.

As Husserl describes it, this form of reflection seems to come into play only as part of the project of phenomenology. Though always presumably a possibility, this most radical form of reflection was never pursued prior to its "discovery" ("invention"?) by Husserl. And as we have seen, Husserl himself describes phenomenological reflection as something highly artificial, a frame of mind or attitude linked with a very special set of theoretical interests.

Is There a Transcendental Subject?

Having formulated the distinction between the two senses of subject in this way, how are we to conceive of the relation between the two?

Are there really two selves? As with Kant, there is a certain presumption of identity. After all, both conceptions result from my reflection upon "myself," presumably the very same self. Two different forms of reflection yield two different descriptions of the self reflected upon. But the identity of the self becomes a problem if the two descriptions are incompatible. And Husserl himself suggests that they are indeed radically incompatible. This is what he calls the "paradox of human subjectivity: being a subject for the world and at the same time being an object in the world" (CR 178). Trying to express it in the most paradoxical way, Husserl writes: "The subjective part of the world swallows up, so to speak, the whole world and thus itself too. What an absurdity!" (CR 180).

In his attempt to resolve this paradox, Husserl makes a distinction we came across in Fichte [see chapter 2, pp. 54–5.]: When I perform the epoche and reflect transcendentally, "I am not a single individual . . . I am not *an* ego, who still has his *you*, his *we*, his total community of cosubjects in natural validity." If this is the genuine sense of "I," that which individualizes me and distinguishes me from others, then this transcendental ego "is actually called 'I' only by equivocation," Husserl says (CR 184). The reason for this is that this "I" distinguishes me from everything else, not just from other subjects. In natural reflection I stand in relation to the human community, again, as part to whole. In transcendental reflection other subjects, indeed the whole community they form, become part of the "phenomenon" of the world that is now considered exclusively as my intended world.[8]

As solution to the paradox, Husserl again turns to the notion of self-constitution: in this instance, the transcendental or "primal" ego constitutes "itself" as empirical or individual ego as one among the *others*. This form of self-constitution would presumably be nothing other than the "natural" reflection we have been speaking about, in which I take myself to be part of the whole that is the natural world and the social world taken together.

But if this is a solution to the "paradox of human subjectivity," it seems to lead in its turn to another paradox, similar in some ways to that encountered already in Kant. In reference to Kant, after distinguishing between transcendental and empirical subjects, we had occasion to ask, *is* there a transcendental subject? With Husserl we could ask the same question. And the answer is similarly ambiguous. On the one hand, Husserl wants to stress the *existence* of the ego in transcendental reflection: "ego sum" provides us with an "apodictically existing basis to stand on" (CM 22). On the other hand, this ego is deprived of any normal sense of existing, that is, being an entity among other entities, existing for an ego as an object within the horizon of the world. As we have seen, this subject is not an individual in any normal sense of the word—it is called "I" "by equivocation only." Yet it is no ideal entity either, not a mere essence, type, or in Husserl's sense an eidos. What kind of entity can be neither real nor ideal, neither particular nor universal, neither an individual nor part of the world?

There is also a sense in which this subject is "empty" or undetermined: as we have seen, as consciousness *of*, it derives its sense from what it is "of." It is nothing but its intentional relation to the world; its only content is the *intentional* content of its objects. But these are not properties or determinations of the transcendental subject; whether they exist or not, they transcend the subject and its intentions; they are in no way to be considered "really inherent parts" of it. Can the transcendental subject exist if it has no properties, parts, or determinations?

These are questions having to do with the *being* of the transcendental subject; similar questions can be raised about its being *known*. It is true that Husserl never says it is unknowable in the sense that Kant's transcendental subect is unknowable; on the contrary, the Cartesian strain in his thinking suggests that it is the most knowable, or most certain, thing of all. Yet the normal conditions for being known—being given as an object within the horizon of the world, being identifiable as having a certain essence and as belonging to a region of being—are not met. Describing my awareness of myself in transcendental reflection as a form of self-knowledge would seem to be "by equivocation only," since it is comparable to no other form of knowledge.

These considerations lead us to pose the same Humean question we did in the last chapter: is the transcendental subject not something rather like a fiction? The idea that the transcendental subject might have something "fictional" about it is strengthened when we recall that this subject seems to emerge only in a very special set of circumstances. It comes to light through self-awareness, of course, or reflection. However, it makes its appearance not in any of the different forms of "natural reflection," but only in the "transcendental reflection" linked with the phenomenological epoche and the transcendental reduction. Only when the world as a whole is bracketed, and acquires the status of the "intended as such," does this purely intentional character of consciousness emerge, and with it the transcendental subject.

Now the phenomenological reduction is a highly specialized mental operation with its own particular theoretical goals and interests. Husserl himself remarks on its "artificial" character, as we have noted, as opposed to the "natural" attitude in which all other forms of reflection are included. Two peculiarities of Husserl's philosophy have always been noted by commentators, both sympathetic and unsympathetic. First, Husserl identifies phenomenology as an intuitive method, one based on the evidence of looking and seeing; yet the extraordinary mental gymnastics of the epoche and reduction, which Husserl never finished clarifying and refining, are required before one can see what there is to see. Second, when the phenomenological method is portrayed as the complete overthrow of our natural belief in the world, one wonders (as in the case of Descartes' doubt) whether something so radical is really possible, or whether Husserl has in mind a "merely" theoretical pretense, a thought experiment which does not really change our beliefs at all.

These considerations suggest that the transcendental subject is indeed something like an imaginative construct, a philosopher's invention, the result of a certain way of looking at things. To be sure, it is not a mere flight of fancy. Rather, it emerges from from a long series of considerations, of the sort we have traced in this chapter. It might be said to have the status of a *theoretical fiction*, comparable, let us say, to the freely falling body of Newtonian physics or the "average consumer" of statistics. That is, it is something required by a certain theory, but not taken to actually exist; indeed, in these cases we take it not to exist. It is, we might say, just the self (the empirical self?) looked at in a highly abstract or artificial way, one required by a highly abstract and artificial method.

Thus it might be said that if the transcendental subject is a fiction, then it is at least, as with Kant, a necessary fiction. But this only pushes the question back one step. The transcendental subject may be required by the method, but is the method itself required? That is, is phenomenology something we have, in any practical or even theoretical sense, to do? To perform the epoche, to suspend the natural attitude, is within our "perfect freedom," Husserl says (ID1 58). But are we required, or indeed even motivated, to do so? According to E. Fink, in a celebrated article explicitly approved by Husserl, the epoche is in no way rationally required by the natural attitude, which is perfectly coherent on its own. The reasons for performing it can only be discerned after it has been performed, from within the phenomenological attitude![9]

All this makes the epoche, and the transcendental subject that emerges through it, seem not merely artificial but even rather arbitrary. One can even call it "unnatural" since it seems a wholly unnecessary departure from that natural attitude that is given beforehand, and which as "natural" seems necessary and unassailable.[10] Of course, we must remember that when Husserl tells us it is within our "perfect freedom" to suspend the natural attitude, he is claiming that this attitude—the

natural attitude—is not necessary either, that is, precisely that our commitment to it can be lifted, in some sense or other, "at will." Yet the
degree to which, and the sense in which, this suspension is really possible, that is, the degree to which we can genuinely leave the natural
attitude behind, has, as we have noted, been questioned by many commentators and even by Husserl himself.

Let us now draw some conclusions regarding the degree to which Husserl is committed to a "metaphysics of the subject."

It should be clear by now that Husserl in no way affirms the existence of the transcendental ego as some sort of basic substance, as that
term is understood in modern (or indeed pre-modern) philosophy. Nor
does he reduce the world to "representations" belonging to this ego as
predicates to subject. The intentional relation of consciousness to world
is not a subject-predicate relation any more than it is a causal relation
for Husserl; the world and its objects *transcend* consciousness in the
sense that they precisely do not belong to it as its parts or properties
in any sense of these terms. Consciousness is consciousness of these
objects and of the world, not of pictures or images of them that reside
in the mind. As we have seen, it was in order to correct this basic error
of modern philosophy that the concept of intentionality was introduced
in the first place.

Still less does Husserl's phenomenology represent any sort of epistemological "foundationalism" in the sense of the modern tradition.
Transcendental subjectivity is not something from which we can deduce
or otherwise infer the existence of the world or the nature of the things
in it; Husserl never claims that we know the world with any more
certainty or accuracy after the phenomenological reduction than before
it. Nor does he solve this problem of foundation in the manner of
German Idealism by overcoming the transcendence of the world
through a synthetic appropriation.[11]

The empirical subject, which Husserl calls an "object in the world,"
is of course a substance in the traditional sense that relates both causally
and intentionally to other things. The status of the transcendental subject, by contrast, and its relation to the empirical subject, are highly
problematic and unclear. The "two subjects" are obviously the same
self, yet they have two seemingly incompatible descriptions. These two
different senses of the subject derive, as we have seen, from two very
different modes of self-consciousness or reflection: natural reflection,
of which there are many forms, and transcendental reflection, which is
linked to the highly specialized and theoretically sophisticated method

of phenomenology. This in turn lends to the transcendental subject the air of something contrived or artificial, something like a theoretical fiction.

The fact that phenomenology is conceived by Husserl as a *method* is of great significance for the question at hand. One reply to the question of whether Husserl's philosophy constitutes a "metaphysics of the subject" is to point out that Husserl claims not to be putting forward a metaphysical doctrine at all but to be engaged in a "working philosophy" (CM 86) instead, that is, to be proposing concrete procedures for analyzing meaning in its various forms. Like Kant's philosophy (and like the positivism of Husserl's contemporaries) phenomenology is not meant to replace old metaphysical doctrines with new ones, but is conceived as a critique of the whole naive, dogmatic project of metaphysics. The point of the method, as we have seen, is neither to deny nor to reaffirm the natural attitude, nor is it to go beyond it to some other realm; it is simply to see, as it were, how the natural attitude "works."

It is this project that consists in performing the epoche and invoking the phenomenological reduction. It is this procedure that requires that we consider the subject purely as intentional, that is, as transcendental. To "ontologize" this subject, to affirm its transcendental characteristics independently of the procedure, would be to replace method with metaphysics.[12]

FOUR

The Self in the Transcendental Tradition

In this chapter I want to draw together the views of Kant and Husserl that have been exposed in the previous two chapters. I shall argue that these two philosophers have very similar things to say about subjectivity and that their views together establish and constitute something that can be understood as a "transcendental tradition." The unity and coherence of this tradition and its place in modern philosophy have not, I have claimed, been sufficiently understood. In particular, as I said at the outset, they have been misunderstood by Heidegger in his sweeping, influential reading of the history of modern philosophy. Thus it will be important, as we try to articulate the nature of the transcendental tradition, to contrast it with the interpretations of Heidegger that have been, to many, so convincing. Once the unity and general contours of this tradition have become visible, I shall attempt to show that other, post-Husserlian thinkers belong to this tradition as well, even if they do not explicitly acknowledge it.

Of course, the historical connection between Husserl and Kant is there to be found, and has been commented on by many, starting with Husserl himself.[1] We have already noted, in the last chapter (p. 82), not only some borrowed terminology—notably, of course, the term "transcendental" itself—but also a number of shared problems and views. While in the *Logical Investigations* Husserl debates primarily with his contemporaries and with the British Empiricists, beginning with the *Ideas* he speaks frequently and positively of Kant and the neo-Kantians. Of course, this is also the point at which Descartes begins to play a major role in his presentations of phenomenology. Husserl makes his indebtedness to Kant explicit in the essay "Kant and the Idea of Transcendental Philosophy" (1924), originally a lecture given at an official commemoration of Kant's 200th birthday.[2] As with Descartes, Husserl conceives of himself as the only thinker who is genuinely fulfilling Kant's intentions, something Kant himself was unable to do. Though he finds much to praise and identify with in both thinkers, his readings of them always contain strong criticisms as well.

In what follows I will not be taking Husserl's views of Kant, positive or negative, or his assessment of his relation to Kant, as my guide, nor will I always emphasize the same things he does in arguing for the unity of the transcendental approach. The ideas I am bringing together here cannot be forged into a single theory or doctrine; they cannot even be described as making up a school or a movement. This is why it may be preferable to speak of a tradition. It can be seen first of all as a path of historical influence arising out of a common attitude toward the philosophical past. It is characterized by a shared recognition and setting of problems, by a common assessment of philosophical priorities. It is possible to assert that the unity is one of method or approach rather than doctrine, but we have seen that the concept of method, so important in modern philosophy since Descartes, has been rendered suspect by Heidegger. Hence, if we are to invoke it we shall have to handle it with care. Above all, in attempting to articulate a coherent "transcendental" conception of the subject, we shall be seeking not so much to work out a single theory as to find a unified approach to a problem that arises within a larger philosophical project.

The Transcendental Project: Critique, Not Metaphysics

What is that project? The question I have raised in introducing my discussions of Kant and Husserl is whether their views can be characterized, as suggested by Heidegger, as a metaphysics of the subject. The first point that must be made in response (and we have already noted this in reference to Kant) is that for both authors, transcendental philosophy is not to be understood as metaphysics at all. In a way, for both thinkers metaphysics is certainly at issue, but precisely for this reason it is not the rubric under which they classify their own work. Kant is explicitly addressing the question of whether metaphysics, as conceived and practiced by his predecessors and contemporaries, is possible at all as a science. What he proposes is a critique of metaphysics, a project that is prepared for by a critique of mathematics and natural science. These disciplines claim in different ways to have knowledge of the world; Kant's task is neither to subscribe to their claims nor to add to them, nor to replace them with claims of his own, but to inquire into how they are possible (see A12/B26).[3] Husserl's phenomenology, likewise, does not consist of knowledge claims about the world, whether scientific or metaphysical. By "bracketing" these claims, as we have seen, he turns his attention from the world and its objects to the experiences in which they are given. Like Kant, he emphasizes the "how" question: the " 'how' of manners of givenness" (CR 165f.).

In sum, both thinkers conceive of themselves not as producing knowledge about reality or the world, but as reflecting on such knowledge, not as saying things about the world but as describing our experience of the world. In their own view they are neither adding to scientific knowledge nor contributing to a specifically philosophical theory of the world that might be called metaphysics. If neither philosopher thinks that he is engaged in metaphysics at all, then a fortiori neither is proposing what he thinks of as a metaphysics of the subject, whether as a metaphysical theory based on the subject or as a metaphysical theory about the subject. In Kant's case, as we have noted, a metaphysics of the subject (in the form of "rational psychology") comes explicitly under his critical gaze, and his distinction between the empirical and the transcendental subject is directly related to this critique. The same can be said of Husserl, as we shall argue later, especially with reference to what he calls the "paradox of human subjectivity."

In seeing themselves not as contributing to knowledge about the world but as reflecting critically on such knowledge, Kant and Husserl take up the modern reflective tradition inaugurated by Descartes and continued by the British Empiricists. According to this tradition, epistemology, in the sense of a critical reflection on knowledge, must come before metaphysics. But these thinkers were operating with a conception of proper philosophical priorities. Descartes believed that the critical question—whether knowledge is possible at all—could be settled, and philosophy could move on to metaphysical questions. For the Empiricists, too, this was the proper order of inquiry, even if their arguments led to the conclusion, finally drawn by Hume, that the assurances about knowledge sought by Descartes could not be had.

Partly under the influence of Hume's skeptical conclusions, Kant and Husserl make a crucial break with this traditional modern conception of philosophical procedure. For them the critical reflection on knowledge is not a prelude to a revived and reassured metaphysics in the old style, that is, in the sense of a science of the world that at once builds upon, goes beyond, and complements the existing sciences. Transcendental philosophy as critical reflection becomes an end in itself rather than a prelude to something else, and its relation to "positive" knowledge of the world is very different from that envisaged by the early moderns. Even though the term "metaphysics" reappears in a positive sense in both thinkers,[4] it is seen not as a subject matter apart from transcendental philosophy but as part of it. For Kant and Husserl, it is fair to say, genuine knowledge about the world, insofar as this is possible, and within its own limits, is to be found in the sciences. For Husserl, though not for Kant, this includes the social, psychological, and humanistic disciplines as well as the natural sciences. Husserl also believes that we have a pre-scientific familiarity, a kind of knowledge by acquaintance, with the world. But there is no further body of knowledge, as in the traditional conception of metaphysics, that goes beyond the sciences, makes up for their deficiencies, and somehow incorporates their results into a grand theory of the whole. The only thing apart from our experiential and scientific knowledge of the world is our critical reflection on it, that is, transcendental philosophy itself, which lies, as Kant suggests,[5] not *beyond* scientific knowledge but on *this side* of it.

As we have seen (chapter 1, p. 14), the idea that critical reflection is distinct from metaphysics, and can be practiced independently of it, is simply not acknowledged by Heidegger. To be sure, I am not claiming that Heidegger is unaware of this crucial distinction in Kant and Husserl, or has simply overlooked their assertions that they are not doing metaphysics at all. He simply flatly denies the distinction, asserting that transcendental philosophy is "the modern form of ontology" (UM 74). Of course, he is hardly the first to challenge this classically modern distinction. He has been preceded most famously by Hegel, notably in the introduction to the *Phänomenologie des Geistes*. Hegel tries to undermine the distinction by asking why the critical reflection on claims to knowledge does not itself count as knowledge. If metaphysics is knowledge of the whole, why is knowledge about knowledge not itself knowledge of part of the whole and thus part of metaphysics? His overall strategy is to point to the many assumptions that underlie any such reflection, assumptions that are arguably themselves metaphysical assumptions.

Hegel's argument is brilliant, though it has hardly commanded universal assent. But it is at least an argument, an internal critique of the whole modern notion of the priority of epistemology over metaphysics. Heidegger, by contrast, offers no argument for his claim that all modern philosophers, Kant and Husserl included, are "really" doing metaphysics, whatever they may say they are doing. It is true that Heidegger devotes a whole essay to a detailed paragraph-by-paragraph analysis of Hegel's introduction to the *Phänomenologie*.[6] But this essay can hardly be read as an endorsement or adoption by Heidegger of Hegel's argument. Indeed, Heidegger's purpose there seems consistent with his treatment of other modern philosophers: he wants to demonstrate that Hegel's thought is yet another manifestation of the modern metaphysics of the subject. His approach is like Hegel's in emphasizing unspoken metaphysical assumptions; but the assumptions he finds in Hegel's text are not those Hegel would recognize, but the same ones he finds everywhere else: the interpretation of the being of beings as subjectivity.

Indeed, we can say it is *Heidegger's* assumption, for which he nowhere gives an argument, that anyone attempting a critique of knowledge, prior to and independently of metaphysics, is actually, but unknowingly, giving expression to a metaphysics. Is this true of Kant and Husserl, contrary to what they think? Should we simply accept Heidegger's view because he states it? No; but we should treat Kant's and Husserl's conception of non-metaphysical transcendental philosophy with the same caution. Charitably, we should treat Heidegger's claim about the relation of transcendental philosophy to metaphysics as a *hypothesis*, supposedly confirmed in his interpretations of the philosophers he treats. Even if we are not convinced by his interpretations, his hypothesis is one worth considering. But equally worth considering is the assumption, or hypothesis, at the heart of transcendental philosophy, that metaphysics can be "bracketed" and subjected to a reflective critique.

Our own procedure here will be to favor that hypothesis, and seek its confirmation in our own interpretations of transcendental philosophy. It is an aspect of the tradition inaugurated by Kant, and continued by Husserl, that has been all too quickly dismissed by Heidegger and his followers, and it needs to be reinstated as a key to the proper understanding of that tradition. In the following I shall be taking seriously this hypothesis. But I shall have to return to it later, after a lengthier exposition of the transcendental project, and to the question of whether it can be sustained in a manner that survives Heidegger's critique.

Representationalism

What does it mean to say that transcendental philosophy is not a meta-physics of the subject but a critique of the metaphysics of the subject? For one thing, it means that transcendental philosophy, as envisaged by both Kant and Husserl, is not a representational theory but precisely a critique of the representational theory. For Heidegger, as we have seen, modern philosophy is characterized by the shift of the traditional notion of substance to the knowing subject. This subject exists not through properties or predicates in the traditional sense but through representations—pictures of objects or a picture of the world as a whole. Heidegger assimilates both Kant and Husserl to this modern tradition, overlooking that the critique of the notion of representation is the very core of their whole project.

Heidegger is certainly right that the notion of representation is cen-tral to the modern tradition and the key to its many problems. He is also right that it results at least in part from considering the mind according to the traditional notion of substance. Also known as the "way of ideas," according to which the mind is directly related only to its own thoughts, the notion of representation closes the mind off from the rest of the world and raises the question of whether knowledge and experience are even possible, and more radically how they should be defined. Once the problem of our relation to the world is set up in this way, it is almost inevitable that the only possible outcomes are skepticism or idealism. Either the gap between ideas and the "external world" can never be bridged at all, or the external world is simply reduced to ideas or representations (as in Leibniz and Berkeley) and itself becomes a property of mind. The latter solution, in which a metaphysical thesis comes to the rescue of an epistemological problem, is the one that interests Heidegger. And it is of this that he accuses both Kant and Husserl in their role as metaphysicians. But in doing so he misunderstands them completely.

It is true that the term *Vorstellung*, which corresponds roughly to the English and French versions of *idea* in early modern philosophy, is central to Kant's theory of knowledge; but as we saw, Kant's approach is new. The problem is that *Vorstellungen* are determinations of the sub-ject or the mind; if the mind relates only to these its own determina-tions, no knowledge is possible, for knowledge must be of objects, that is, must be about the world. Agreeing with Hume that neither reason alone nor sense experience (in the empiricist sense) could ever guar-antee the connection between ideas and things, Kant concluded that the connection must be a priori: his answer is precisely the transcendental unity of apperception, conceived as the *objective* unity of self-consciousness (B139) relating the "I think" through representations to objects. It is not to be derived from experience, but is a condition of the possibility of experience, that the "I think" accompany all my representations and in doing so relate them to objects. It will be recalled from chapter 2 that the role of the transcendental unity of apperception is not only to unify the manifold of experiences in the subject a priori, but also to unify them in an object, and this equally a priori. In other words, as we saw, the "I think" is transitive or intentional.

It is important to understand Kant's use of the terms "a priori" and "transcendental" when he applies them to the "I think," the unity of apperception, and the relation of representations to an object. He is saying that these constitute the very essence of experience, and that philosophically we cannot expect to derive them from anything simpler or more basic. Kant's starting point is that "we are in possession" of certain cognitions, which means that we *have* experience, in his full sense of that term. This starting point is as much the key to his role in modern philosophy as the notion of the "Copernican Revolution." Indeed, it is another way of looking at it. It is Kant's response to Descartes' starting point and the Humean skepticism to which it ultimately leads. Instead of starting with the encapsulated mind and then asking how we get out of it to the world, we must begin with a notion of mind that is already (i.e., a priori) outside of itself and in the world.

Kant calls the unity of apperception the "supreme principle of all employment of the understanding" (B136). Thus he places it even above the categories. His argument for the unity of apperception is similar to that for the categories, but it must come first. His argument for causality, for example, is that it cannot be derived from experience, and without it experience would not be possible. Hence it must be considered a priori and transcendental, a condition of the possibility of experience. But causal relations are relations among objects, not representations. Hence the objective (i.e., intentional) character of experience establishes in general the realm to which the categories apply. Objectivity alone, of course, is not enough, so certain features of the objective realm, like causal interaction and regularity, must be considered a priori as well. But without the objective aspect of the unity of apperception, there would be nothing—that is, no world of objects—to which the categories could apply.

As we have seen (chapter 3, p. 71), not only is Husserl not a representationalist; the impetus for his entire development can be found in his early attack, in the *Logical Investigations*, on the notion of mental representation. This is what we called (p. 72) the "realist" element in his early work and is of a piece with his attack on psychologism—that is, on the attempt to collapse the object of consciousness into consciousness or to confuse the two. Like Kant, he places the objective relation—intentionality—in first place, recognizing that it is essential to experience and that it cannot be derived from anything more primitive.

In this respect Husserl's starting point is the same as Kant's, but he expresses it in a different way. Husserl does not present an argument based on the inadequacy of mental representations to secure the objective relation, but rather shows that the idea of such representation cannot be backed up by a phenomenological description. In *Ideas* 1 he devotes a whole section (ID1 43) to what he calls the "fundamental error" of believing that perception "does not reach the physical thing itself" but only a picture of it, or perhaps a sign or symbol for it. We understand perfectly well what it is to see a picture (say a photograph of my house), which "stands in" for something else and genuinely represents it, and how that differs from seeing "in person" or "in the flesh" (*leibhaftig*) the thing it represents. Here the very concept of a representation presupposes the idea of direct seeing, indeed doubly so, since a) the depicted object is something that *could* be seen directly, and b) the picture itself *is* seen directly, in contrast to the thing it depicts. In spite of being "transcendent," in the sense of belonging to "reality" as distinct from consciousness, the object of perception (see ID1. section 42) is present, directly given to the perceiver as itself.

For Husserl it is not just the object of perception but "reality" as a whole, indeed the *world*, that transcends consciousness. But consciousness is not somehow cut off from this transcendence; on the contrary, it is *as* transcendent that object and world are given, indeed directly given, to consciousness. This is possible because consciousness is nothing that could be cut off from the world: as intentionality it is nothing but this relation to the world. As we have seen, for Husserl, the fact that consciousness thus transcends itself is what gives transcendental philosophy its name. Kant does not give us a similar account of his choice of the term, nor does he use the term "transcendent" in the way that Husserl does. But it is clear that he begins with the assumption, and never doubts, that we *have* experience of the objective world, and that he sees his own task as that of showing how this is possible.

For both thinkers, then, the starting point is that the world is both objective and given. The historical importance of this starting point cannot be emphasized too much. For pre-Kantian modern philosophers, and even for some post-Kantians, these two features exclude one another: what is objective cannot be given; what is given is subjective and cannot be objective. Kant and Husserl are determined to show how the two go together.

In Husserl's phenomenology of perception, the perceived is given only one-sidedly or perspectivally, subject to the general conditions of perception. This one-sidedness is not a hindrance to the givenness of things; it is not an "appearance" or "representation" standing between us and the objects. On the contrary, it is our very mode of access to them. For Kant, too, objects are given to us subject to the conditions of both sensibility and the understanding—space, time, and the categories. This is just the "how" of their givenness. The overarching condition, as we have seen, is the transcendental unity of apperception. But this principle just describes the essential character of consciousness itself, precisely as consciousness of the world. It simply says that if the world is to be given, we must be conscious of it. As we saw in the last chapter, Kant's search for the conditions of the possibility of experience is first of all the attempt to state what experience is, that is, to lay bare its basic structure, or, as he puts it, the *form* of thinking (*die Form des Denkens* [A93/B126]). We can now see how close this is to the Husserlian project of phenomenological description as the description of the *essence* of consciousness, of objectivity, of world.

Thus we must stress the givenness of the objective world, in both thinkers, in order to counter the charge that their position is a representationalist one. But it is also important, in our interpretation of the transcendental tradition, to stress the world's transcendence (in Husserl's sense) or objectivity (in Kant's sense). This is a feature of the tradition that is often underplayed, since it seems to run counter to the original insight that gets the whole thing going. Kant's great innovation, after all, is the idea that the mind, instead of passively mirroring an independent and self-sufficient reality, is active and productive. Kant describes it as "prescribing laws to nature, and even of making nature possible" (B159f). Husserl's term is "constitution," and both thinkers describe consciousness as synthesis.

But constitution is not creation; synthesis does not manufacture the world. As Kant says, the understanding "does not produce its object as far as its *existence* is concerned" (A92/B125). For Kant this means that our intellect is finite. It is often thought that the mark of this finitude is the role played by sense in his theory. Indeed, Kant speaks of sensation as the raw material that is shaped and fashioned by the understanding (A1). The early Husserl, too, employs the notion of hyletic data brought to life by an animating intention. But if this were the only sense of finitude, they would indeed come close to the blasphemous "humanism" that seems to be the true source of Heidegger's critique: as if human reason replaced God in all but the creation of prime matter.

In fact, the metaphor of matter formed by the mind is very misleading in both thinkers. The unformed matter of sensation is not, for either of these philosophers, the genuine mark of human finitude or the sense of the world's transcendence. If in transcendental philosophy the mind does not create the world, it is not because some kernel of uncreated, pre-given stuff is required for the mix. It is because what the mind genuinely does produce is not existence but meaning. And the primary meaning it generates is that of the objectivity or transcendence of the world. The attempt to absorb that transcendence into subjectivity, in the manner of Leibniz or Berkeley, or even of Fichte and Hegel, would be for Kant and Husserl to confuse meaning with being. Furthermore, the meaning generated by subjectivity is itself finite in the sense that it does not exhaust all the possibilities of being.

Transcendental Idealism: Doctrine or Method?

Both Kant and Husserl characterize their position as transcendental idealism, and both are concerned to distinguish this position from realism *and* idealism in the usual sense. Realism and idealism are both metaphysical theories about reality and its relation to the mind. The danger here is to think that transcendental idealism is some third metaphysical position, perhaps somehow combining the other two. Both Kant and Husserl have often been considered in this way, even by their most sympathetic commentators. Kant is often characterized as affirming both the reality of the mind-independent world (things in themselves) and the merely mental character of the objects of our experience (appearances). Husserl, who rejects Kant's notion of the thing-in-itself (see CM 156), is more often characterized simply as an idealist who "reduces" the real world to mental phenomena, and this in spite of the fact that he apparently wants to hold a direct-realist theory of perception. As metaphysicians, Kant and Husserl do not come off very well. Transcendental idealism, considered as a metaphysical theory, seems not to be very coherent.

But a great deal of sense can be made of transcendental idealism if it is taken not as a metaphysical alternative to or mixture of realism and idealism, but as a critical reflection on experience, science, and metaphysics, a reflection on the form or essence of experience that is situated at a different level from metaphysical concerns. H. Allison points out that Kant in one place speaks of "formal" as opposed to "material" idealism (B 519n.) and wishes he had stuck to this terminology. For Allison, Kant is reflecting on the "limits and conditions of human knowledge," that is, on the *form* of consciousness, "not on the contents of consciousness or the nature of *an sich* reality."[7]

This formulation permits us to see more clearly the affinity between Kant's transcendental idealism and Husserl's, not only as a search for the essence or structure of experience, but also as a reflection that brackets the existence of the objects of experience. Both thinkers could be said to be concerned with the objects of experience, but from a particular point of view, namely, not straightforwardly or directly, that is, not as they are "in themselves," but as they appear, with respect to the conditions and characteristics of their appearance. Husserl's "bracketing" procedure has its origin in a distinction he makes in the *Logical Investigations* between *"the object as it is intended [der Gegenstand, so wie er intendiert ist]* and simply the *object which* is intended [und schlecthin der Gegenstand, welcher intendiert ist]"* (LI 578, modified translation). Phenomenology is concerned with objects, but only insofar as, and with respect to how or under what conditions, they are intended. Anything about the object that lies outside this consideration, whatever it may be above and beyond the way it is intended, is simply placed out of consideration or bracketed. The "object as" of the *Logical Investigations* becomes the "noema" of *Ideas* 1 and the *cogitatum qua cogitatum* of the *Cartesian Meditations*. To bracket the object-which, the object *"schlecthin"* or "in itself," is not to deny it or to doubt it is there, it is just to turn our attention away from it and toward its manners of givenness. If Husserl had seen Kant's thing-in-itself not as some mysterious separate entity, posited metaphysically behind appearances (the standard caricature), but simply as the bracketed object-which, he would not have criticized it as he did.

To sum up, Kant's thing-in-itself and Husserl's bracketed object and world are just the straightforwardly, naively taken-for-granted reality of our pre-reflective experience, from which we must turn away if we are to reflect critically on our experience. Kant's appearances, and Husserl's *noemata* or *cogitata qua cogitata*, are just those very same objects considered from a critical-reflective point of view—that is, with respect to how they are intended and under what conditions they appear.[8]

Emphasizing the role of critical reflection, and the point of view that goes with it, in these distinctions, permits us to conceive of transcendental idealism, indeed transcendental philosophy, not as a set of claims or theses but as a procedure, or "research program," in today's parlance. For Kant the key word is *critique*: "this enquiry," he says in introducing his major work and justifying its title, ". . . should be entitled not a doctrine but only a transcendental critique" (A12/B26). Husserl says that transcendental idealism "*is* nothing more than a consequentially executed self-explication," a "*sense-explication* achieved *by actual work*" (CM 86). P. Ricoeur, describing Husserl's procedure, speaks of a "methodological rather than a doctrinal idealism."[9] In other words, Husserl proposes only that we *consider* the world exclusively as phenomenon, purely as sense for us, rather than *asserting* that it is nothing but phenomenon, nothing but sense. For him this proposal is formulated in the idea of the phenomenological epoche and reduction.

Husserl's proposal is that the philosopher suspend the "natural attitude" and take up the phenomenological attitude instead. It is in the natural attitude that the ontological status of the world is asserted or believed in; it is in the sciences of the natural attitude that questions of "what there is" are decided. The natural attitude consists of ontological assumptions about the world ("in itself") and experiences and judgments (both scientific and everyday) in which those assumptions are filled in or made concrete. As I have been insisting, the purpose of phenomenological description (or transcendental critique) is not to deny those assumptions, or to question those experiences or judgments, but merely to understand them. The phenomenological attitude does not replace the natural attitude, as we saw, but only brackets it, the better to understand it. Consequently there is a sense in which it never leaves the natural attitude behind, but constantly returns it in the "zig-zag" pattern Husserl often refers to.

A passage from the *Crisis* will clarify what I mean. What Husserl calls the "mathematization of nature," which is the key to the success of science since Galileo, is actually a method, "designed for the purpose of progressively improving, *in infinitum* . . . , those rough predictions which are the only ones originally possible within the sphere of . . . the life-world." (CR 51f). The method is to treat the natural world as a purely mathematical realm by considering only those features of it that are susceptible to precise mathematical measurement. The philosophers, however, have converted this methodological procedure into an ontological thesis: they "take for *true being* what is actually a *method*" (CR 51). To be is to be mathematically measurable.

Something similar occurs if phenomenological investigation (or transcendental critique) is converted into straightforward idealism. The methodological injunction to treat the world purely in terms of its sense, or the conditions of its appearance, is converted into the claim that it is nothing but its sense or its appearance. This would be precisely to "take for *true being* what is actually a method," to convert a procedure into an ontological thesis that by no means follows from it.

The Question of Method

To insist that transcendental philosophy is method and not metaphysics,[10] however, forces us to consider critically the notion of method itself, and to face up to some of Heidegger's critical remarks on this concept. The combination of subjectivity and method, it will be recalled, is for Heidegger one of the key features of modern philosophy as a whole, beginning with Descartes. Cartesian method, mathematical-deductive method, scientific or experimental method—all are so many expressions, according to Heidegger, of the relation of mastery and control between subject and world. The crucial central role of method in modern philosophy and science demonstrates for Heidegger that the concept of the subject, beginning with Descartes, is intimately tied to the notion of "enframing" the world through technological domination.

This would hold true of Husserl and Kant only if the point of their method was really to "reduce" the world to appearances. But we know that this is not what transcendental idealism means in Kant: the idea of the thing-in-itself prohibits us from thinking that there is nothing to the world but what can be captured in our scientific categories. And it should be clear that this is not what "reduction" means in Husserl, and indeed that the term was poorly chosen. What the reduction does is reveal the meaning-aspect of the world that we naively take for granted. This aspect of Heidegger's criticism will apply to Husserl and Kant only if he succeeds, as he tries so hard to do, in including them in the historical sweep of idealism that begins with Descartes, culminates in Hegel, and then is articulated as will to power by Nietzsche. If our interpretation is correct, the two transcendental philosophers must be regarded not as part of this historical development, but as exceptions to it who are indeed struggling against it.

They do this, however, as we have seen, not by opting for realism but by trying to overcome this tired opposition and move beyond such metaphysical disputes. Of this Heidegger should approve. Indeed, it is one of the genuine merits of Heidegger's account of the history of modern philosophy that by tying idealism and technology together he argues in effect that there is little to choose between modern idealism and realism. The latter, after all, at least as "scientific realism," has conceived of reality as precisely that realm of measurable entities and relations that is susceptible to our prediction and control. In other words, realism is reductionist, its "reality" a correlate of human projection and power. This is a genuine phenomenological insight, one that has been pursued by such thinkers as Foucault,[11] which comes not from worrying whether reality is really "out there" or not, but from reflecting on the sense it has in our scientific practices. Husserl and Kant, likewise, must be seen not as endorsing or denying a scientific conception of the word, but as trying to understand its meaning, and as devising a philosophical method that will allow that meaning to emerge.

Another way of talking about the methodological character of transcendental reflection is to say that its purpose is not to arrive at claims about the world, but to acquire a certain point of view on the world, a new way of looking at it. Husserl opposes the natural *attitude* to the phenomenological, and the word he uses, *Einstellung*, could also be translated as "standpoint," or "point of view." As Husserl often says (see ID1 61), phenomenology does not deny the world or even doubt it, much less forsake it to go off somewhere else. Indeed it deals with the very same world that has occupied us all along, in the natural attitude; it just looks at it from a very special point of view, that is, with respect to its manners of givenness. The purpose of the method—epoche, reduction, and so forth—is just to establish or attain that point of view.

There is another, more subtle problem with the concept of method, however, which is sometimes evident in Heidegger's criticism, though not so explicitly so. What we are attributing to Husserl and Kant, as the genuine sense of transcendental philosophy, is the idea of a philosophical method that is metaphysically neutral. Any such method may nevertheless be suspected or accused of harboring metaphysical presuppositions. Heidegger's approach to most of the modern philosophers he writes about is to claim that they are giving expression to a "metaphysische Grundstellung" (ZW 91) in spite of themselves, that their epistemology or other inquiries make sense only because of the metaphysical position they tacitly hold. This approach, though never very explicit as an argumentative strategy in Heidegger, is something very close to the concept of internal or immanent critique. This, it will be recalled, was the strategy employed by Hegel in his critique of the whole epistemological approach of his modern predecessors. This strategy is used explicitly against Husserl by Jacques Derrida. "Do not phenomenological necessity, the rigor and subtlety of Husserl's analysis, nonetheless conceal a metaphysical presupposition?" This is the ques-

tion with which he begins his *Speech and Phenomena,* whose purpose is
to provide an affirmative answer.[12]

Heidegger and Derrida both seem to suggest that such presuppositions are inevitable, that we cannot avoid being part of the metaphysics
of our age. The same point could be made in a quite formal way: Can
any method really stand on its own, without theoretical commitments
or underpinnings? What, exactly, is a method? Simply put, it is a set of
prescriptions for getting from A to B, from some starting point to
some destination. Do not these prescriptions depend on the *theoretical*
claim that A and B are really related in a certain way?

It is an interesting irony that, among those who answer this question
in the affirmative, we find Edmund Husserl himself. Of course, he
makes the point with reference not to phenomenology but to logic.
The first conception of logic he addresses in the "Prolegomena to Pure
Logic" is the one that treats it strictly as a normative discipline or
technique (*Kunstlehre*) for how to think correctly. Husserl argues at
length that logic or any discipline so conceived cannot stand alone.
"Every normative discipline," he writes, "demands that we know certain non-normative truths . . ." (LI 88).

This point may not apply, however, to a method whose purpose is
to reflect critically on the very metaphysical presuppositions that are at
issue. To be sure, any such critique may in fact operate under just the
sort of hidden assumptions that Heidegger and Derrida have in mind,
and anyone is free to try to root them out, just as Heidegger and
Derrida have done. But to assert that any critique must in principle
have and be unaware of such presuppositions is something else. For
one thing, it would apply to, and thus presumably call into question,
Heidegger's and Derrida's critiques as well. But the larger point to be
made is that the critical enterprise is a *self*-critical undertaking that is
constantly reflecting on its own presuppositions with a view to bracketing and understanding them. It is a never-ending process of critical
self-reflection *that is not designed to come to a stopping place with the assertion
of some metaphysical theory.* This is no doubt what Husserl meant by calling
himself a perpetual beginner in philosophy.

This is what I meant by saying that metaphysics was certainly *at issue*
in transcendental philosophy, though it is not itself metaphysics. It is
in the deepest sense a critique of metaphysics for both Kant and Husserl. Kant made the point that by this he did not mean a critique of
books and systems. (B27). He meant instead a critique of those deeply
held beliefs toward which reason itself inclines us in its demand for
ultimate rational satisfaction. Likewise, Husserl discovers and unearths

those profound and fundamental, but taken-for-granted and unre-flected, convictions (*Urglaube*) that make up the natural attitude—the ultimate metaphysics. Both thinkers realize that traditional philosophy—metaphysics—arises out of the structure of human experience. But their approach to it is not to contribute further to it but to reflect critically on its origins.

The Two Egos

Thus transcendental philosophy is anything but a representational the-ory, and transcendental idealism is not a metaphysical thesis. Its focus is intentionality or the transcendental unity of apperception—that is, the relation of experience to the transcendent or objective world. It does not take up this relation in order to affirm it or deny it, to reduce it to something else or to derive it from something else. It simply asks how it is possible or how it works. In exploring this relation, one of the results both Husserl and Kant come upon is the distinction between the empirical and the transcendental subject. In the previous two chap-ters, in examining their views on this topic, I have tried to demystify this distinction and explain how it functions in the context of their theories. It is time to bring these views together and explain how they relate to the whole question of the "metaphysics of the subject."

To begin with intentionality or the experience-world relation is to assume a subject of experience (the "I think") whose whole function is to stand in a meaning-bestowing or (to use Husserl's term) "consti-tuting" relation to the world. Here the primary distinction is between meaning-bestowal and meaning bestowed, or constituting and consti-tuted. As we saw, the "I" in this relation is not the "I" of personal identity that distinguishes me from other persons, but the "I" of sub-jectivity that distinguishes me from everything else, the world as a whole. As Husserl says, the transcendence of the world means that "neither the world nor any worldly Object is a piece of my Ego, to be found in my conscious life as a really inherent part of it, as a complex of data of sensation or a complex of acts" (CM 26). But by the same token, the "I" is not "a piece of the world" either, but a condition of its very possibility—its possibility not as existing, of course, but as meaning.

At the same time we realize that there is an obvious sense in which the "I" *is* part of the world. Reflecting in the natural way, I take myself to be a person among persons, even a thing among things, an object both for myself and others, alongside the other objects in the world.

As we have seen, especially in connection with Husserl's analyses in *Ideas* 2, it is not as if intentionality is excluded when the subject is considered in this way: I as person am one who thinks, perceives, and acts, and who in doing so relates to a natural and social world of meanings and complexes of meaning. But at the same time I am related in other, non-intentional ways to the world. As body I am in space and relate to other bodies in objective space. The events of my life, both bodily and mental, are in objective time and as such relate temporally to other worldly events. And above all these events in my life belong to the causal order of the world and stand in relations of causal dependence and regularity to the things and events in my surroundings.

It is here that the self is simply one item among others in the world, different in many respects from other things but like them in being a grammatical or metaphysical subject (in the sense of substance) with its predicates or properties. It is thus quite "natural" (as in Husserl's natural attitude) that philosophers should have had recourse to the notion of substance in treating the self. But this had led them to include it in a general metaphysics of substance that has raised more problems than it has solved. Kant and Husserl both address themselves to these problems, and it is here that their critique of the metaphysics of substance comes into play. If experiences, thoughts, and ideas are conceived as properties of the self, how do they relate to the objects and the world they are about? The answer is usually a confused mixture of causality and resemblance, which come together in the problematic notion of representation. As we have already noted, posing the question in this way sets up a barrier between self and world that cannot be bridged, and the result is either a skepticism that gives up on knowledge altogether or an idealism that reduces the rest of the world to the ideas we have of it. The first denies the openness to the world that is constitutive of our being as subjects; the second denies the transcendence of the world that is an ineradicable feature of its sense.

In both Kant and Husserl, the distinction between transcendental and empirical subject is introduced as a response to this situation. It expresses their view that both aspects of subjectivity—being subject for the world and being an object in the world—must be recognized, that neither can be effaced in favor of the other. The problem is that their distinction has been misunderstood, for example, by Heidegger, as just another metaphysical doctrine. In particular, it has been taken as following the idealist rather than the skeptical alternative, with the transcendental subject playing the role of ultimate substance, while the world, including the empirical ego, is reduced to a mere representation. This is to construe the distinction as if it were between the real and the merely phenomenal subject, as if there really were two distinct egos with entirely different features and metaphysical status. But as we have seen, both philosophers are clearly speaking about one and the same subject and suggesting that different contexts require radically differing descriptions of that same subject. Neither believes that one of the two descriptions can simply be eliminated in favor of the other, or that one is of something real and the other of something merely apparent.

We have seen that there are various ways of characterizing these different descriptions. All of them have something to do with the type of relations that obtain between the subject and the world of objects— keeping in mind, of course, that intentionality is not a "relation" in the strict sense of the term. Husserl speaks of subject for the world versus object in the world. We can describe the relations between subject and world as purely intentional relations as opposed to (objective) spatial, temporal, and causal relations. We can appeal to the distinction between belonging to the world of objects and being a condition of the possibility of the world of objects (as meaning). Perhaps the broadest terms for these relations would be the *transcendental* relation and the *part-whole* relation. "Transcendental" here is used in both the Kantian and Husserlian senses, which are not quite identical. Kant usually uses the term to refer to something that functions as the condition of the possibility of experience. Husserl uses it to indicate the relation of subjectivity to the transcendence of the world. As for the part-whole relation, the whole in question can be a spatial and temporal whole as well as a causal whole, that is, a causal order.

Subject, Never Object?

Another way of distinguishing transcendental and empirical subjects might appeal to the concepts of subjectivity and objectivity themselves, or even the grammatical distinction between the "I" and the "me." This might be suggested by Husserl's distinction between "subject for" and "object in" the world. That is, we might say that the empirical subject emerges when the reflective gaze is turned upon it; not only does it become an object of the gaze, but in doing so it takes on the primary features of objectivity in general: that of being "out there" in the world, among other objects, and of course among other persons as well. Here it might be said that I become an object for myself just as I am for other people, or even that I am aware of myself in just the way others are aware of me. To reflect in this way is to take the point of view of another on myself, or alternatively to see myself as if I were another.

The transcendental subject, by contrast, might be considered the subject that can never become object. Husserl speaks of it as "indeclinable" (CR 185), meaning that it can never become a "you" or a "he" or a "she," much less a "him" or "her." As Kant puts it (A346/B404), "any judgment upon [the transcendental "I"] has already made use of its representation." Similarly, "The subject of the categories cannot by thinking the categories acquire a concept of itself as an object of the categories. For in order to think them, its pure self-consciousness, which is what was to be explained, must itself be presupposed" (B422). The transcendental subject is as elusive as it is necessary, in other words, since if we try to make it an object it must be an object *for* the subject, and it is this latter subject we are after. Trying to grasp it is like trying to jump over your own shadow, or trying to see your eyes seeing. As I have noted, it is this sort of consideration that led Kant to the view that the transcendental "I" cannot be known, since no intuition of it can be given.

The problem with this way of making the distinction is that the transcendental subject obviously is an object, at least in the sense that we can speak meaningfully about it, describe its characteristics, and distinguish it from the empirical subject. Here Kant faces the same reproach that is often made of his concept of the thing-in-itself: he claims we cannot know it, yet says we know that it exists. Here, too, Kant seems to limit knowing to the empirical knowledge based on sense intuition; we arrive at the thing-in-itself, and apparently at the transcendental subject as well, not from any intuition but as the conclusion of an argument about the conditions of the possibility of experience. In the case of things-in-themselves we may know nothing but that they exist; but in the case of the transcendental subject, by contrast, we have the whole complex Kantian account of its functions as evidence that we are hardly in the dark about it. Why not call this knowledge, and why not admit that the transcendental subject is the object of this knowledge?

This is precisely the question Husserl often addresses to Kant. He describes Kant's account of transcendental subjectivity as "mythical constructions" (CR 114) that result from the fact that Kant did not recognize or admit the possibility of a "transcendental reflection" with its own, legitimate form of intuition. He believes that Kant took all reflection to be based on inner sense and thus to be empirical, and hence merely psychological and unworthy of transcendental philosophy.

Husserl thinks that if Kant had only advanced to the stage of conceiving the phenomenological reduction, he would have recognized that reflection can take itself out of the realm of the empirical and psychological, and become transcendental. And with the transcendental-phenomenological attitude comes a genuinely transcendental experience and intuition. Thus for Husserl "it is in no way correct to assert that the pure Ego is a subject that can never become an Object, as long as we do not limit the concept of Object at the very outset and in particular do not limit it to 'natural' Objects, to mundane 'real' Objects ..." (ID2 107).

Yet as Husserl readily admits, the manner in which the transcendental subject becomes an object is unique, so different from the givenness of any other object that Kant might well be justified in claiming that it would be wrong to compare it to experience at all or to describe it as a form of intuition. Because the "I" of transcendental subjectivity is not *in* the world, it does not situate itself in relation to other objects and cannot be said to obey the rules applicable to objects, at least not in the way that worldly objects do. This, of course, is what Kant means by saying it is not an object of (i.e., is not "subject to") the categories. But even if we object, with Husserl, that Kant's categorial scheme is too narrow, too restrictive in its notion of what kinds of objects there are, clearly there is a sense in which Husserl has the same problem. For him the givenness of any object is always a function of the regional essence or ontology to which it belongs, and these ontological regions belong to the world as a whole. When Husserl "discovers" transcendental consciousness through the reduction, he first describes it as a "new region of being." But I have already explored the difficulties of this conception (see chapter 3, p. 79ff): transcendental consciousness is properly characterized neither as merely one region alongside the others (because it *intentionally* takes them all in) nor as the region of all regions (because it does not "ontologically" or "really" contain them at all). It is considerations of this sort that doubtless led Husserl to stop speaking of consciousness as a "new region of being." And it is what led us to say in the last chapter that it is not at all clear in what sense, for Husserl, the transcendental subject is an object of knowledge at all.

There is of course another sense in which the transcendental subject, when it becomes an "object," is not comparable to any other object. It is directly accessible, namely, to itself alone. It emerges when I reflect on myself in a certain way, distinguishing myself and my intentional, meaning-bestowing consciousness from the meaningful world as a whole. It is, as we might say, a reflection *on* the first-person point of view, *from* the first-person point of view, a point of view I share, by definition, with no one else. The empirical subject, by contrast, is myself as experienced by others as well as myself, the public "me." As we have noted, here I view myself as if I were another. Of course, what Husserl calls "natural reflection," and what Kant calls empirical self-consciousness, is also reflection or self-awareness; and it is only *as if* I were another looking at myself. I still have a direct access to my thoughts, experiences, and intentions that others do not have. But because I take myself to be *in* the world, not merely intentionally but also really and causally related to my surroundings, there is much about me that is important to my being and my behavior that is not directly available to my self-consciousness. For example, my physiological and neurological makeup, my hidden psychological states and dispositions, my character and temperament are all aspects of me that I am aware of, or can become aware of, in myself. They all figure in the view of myself that I have in natural reflection. But I do not come to know them any differently from the way others come to know them in me; and in these respects others may certainly know me better than I know myself.

We must conclude from all this that the transcendental subject is not exactly a subject that can never become object; but the manner in which it becomes an object and its status *as* an object of reflection have still not been adequately described in a general way. Such a description is needed by my own exposition, which seeks to bring together the insights of Kant and Husserl, partly because these points are unclear in the works of the philosophers themselves. The problems encountered in this regard should at least confirm my claim that Kant and Husserl are not simply making metaphysical assertions about the existence of a substantial transcendental subject and reducing the rest of the world to its representations. At most they are both convinced that the subject must be described differently from different points of view. But the question is: what are these points of view, and how do they help us understand the concept of the subject in the transcendental tradition?

The Transcendental Subject as
Theoretical Fiction

More precisely, what is the point of view from which the transcendental subject comes into view? What Kant calls empirical self-consciousness, and what Husserl calls natural reflection, is readily understood, even though much can be said about it. It is just the ordinary self-directed

gaze that takes place in everyday life and that can under some circumstances serve as the basis for certain kinds of self-knowledge. But why
do both philosophers insist that there is another form of self-consciousness? Can we describe that form of reflection in a way that takes
in both Kant's and Husserl's pronouncements? And most important of
all, what does this form of reflection tell us about the status of the
transcendental subject?

Husserl's position is in some ways clearest on this matter. As we
have seen, he distinguishes between natural and transcendental reflection, and the latter is possible only through the phenomenological epoche (CM 72). It is only when our naive, straightforward belief in the
existence of the transcendent world is bracketed, so that its meaning-
structure as constituted comes into view, that the role of consciousness
and the subject as meaning-*constituting* can be appreciated. Only then
can the intentional relation to the world be fully understood in all its
ramifications. Husserl indeed believes that transcendental subjectivity
can be given intuitively, but like any other form of intuition this one
presupposes a general framework, corresponding to a particular "attitude" (*Einstellung*).

This explains the much-quoted footnote on this topic in the second
(1913) edition of the *Logical Investigations*. In the first edition (1901),
Husserl had declared that, search as he might, he was "quite unable to
find" what the Kantians called the "pure ego." But then in the 1913
footnote we are told that subsequent researches had turned it up after
all (LI 459). If we did not know the context, we might imagine Husserl
as a David Hume, searching diligently among his experiences, looking
for one called EGO, coming up empty-handed, then looking harder
and harder until he finally found it. What really happened, of course,
is that in 1901 Husserl had no fully worked-out phenomenological
method, and in 1913 he had worked it out in explicit detail. It was not
a question of looking harder but of looking differently, of having a new
way of looking, which was precisely the method.

Thus it is the phenomenological attitude itself, as distinguished from
all forms of the natural attitude, that makes the intuition of the transcendental subject possible. The phenomenological attitude is circum-
scribed by a set of theoretical goals and expressed in a philosophical
method for reaching those goals. As the contrast with the "naturalness"
of the natural attitude suggests, and as Husserl admits in several places
(LI 254, ID2 189), the phenomenological attitude goes against the grain
of our normal way of looking at things: it is "unnatural" and even
"artificial." It was these considerations that led us to suggest that there
is something contrived about transcendental subjectivity, that it has the

a status of something introduced only in order to serve certain methodological purposes.

Is there anything corresponding to this in Kant? How does the transcendental subject come into view, and on what presuppositions, if any, does it depend? It is, of course, in the context of the "transcendental deduction of the pure concepts of the understanding" that the distinction between empirical and transcendental self-consciousness is first made. Kant's purpose is to show how the categories work to make experience, and finally empirical knowledge, possible. It is all part of the larger project of transcendental philosophy, or rather critique, as an inquiry into the conditions of the possibility of experience and into the question whether metaphysics is possible.

Like Husserl's project, Kant's is an elaborate program of reflection that differentiates itself from science, mathematics, and traditional philosophy. As his famous comparison with Copernicus' revolution in astronomy shows (Bxvi f.), Kant, like Husserl, thought of his project as running counter to our normal way of thinking. Above all, the *question* was new, and again it can be contrasted with Hume's question. Instead of looking for everything in experience, we should ask after the conditions of the possibility of experience. Of course the "I think" will not turn up in experience, he tells Hume, because it belongs to those conditions of experience. In fact, it is chief among them. Thus only by pursuing a philosophical project with a particular set of questions are we brought to the point of recognizing the transcendental subject and its role in experience.

In both philosophers, then, transcendental subjectivity emerges thanks to a deliberate theoretical move away from our "natural" way of seeing ourselves. As our discussion in the previous chapters indicate, we are led by these considerations to think of the transcendental subject as a kind of theoretical fiction, something posited in the context of a theory by the theoretician in order to account for certain things that need an account, but something that has no function or meaning outside the context of the theory. As such, it could be compared to certain concepts in classical physics (the inertial motion of Newton's first law), social science (the average consumer), or the law ("legal fictions" like the corporation treated as a person). In a certain way it makes no sense to ask whether such things exist or whether they can be known: after all, we (or somebody, sometime) just made them up! What is more, everyone who uses these concepts knows that they are fictitious: no one supposes that an inertial motion ever occurs, or goes in search of the average consumer, or asks what a corporation eats for breakfast. No one, in other words, would impute any ontological status to these concepts. Yet they are useful and meaningful within the context of their respective domains.

With these considerations we are brought to the point again where we must take up the "ontological status" of the transcendental subject, a topic we treated in the two previous chapters by asking the question "Is there a transcendental subject?" When the idea of fiction suggests itself, we are put in mind of Hume's use of this concept in connection with the self, and we know that Kant opposed Hume's fictionalism. Husserl opposed it, too (see CR 86ff.). Nevertheless, the idea of the transcendental self as fiction (transcendental fiction?), already discussed in connection first with Kant and then with Husserl, needs now to be explored more thoroughly in a general way.

We have seen that the transcendental subject is elusive and difficult to characterize, hardly an object for us at all in any ordinary sense. All that really emerges from the discussions of Kant and Husserl is a certain *description* of an intentional, spontaneous activity of synthesis or constitution. I have argued that this description is at odds with another description that emerges from our ordinary reflection on ourselves, that of the so-called empirical self. The empirical self is quite "natural," while the transcendental subject seems to be suggested to us by some very complex philosophical considerations and seems to make little sense outside a certain methodological framework. Furthermore, the empirical subject has its place firmly in the world, whereas there is literally no place in the world for the transcendental subject as conceived by Kant and Husserl.

Why not say, then, that in the end the transcendental subject is nothing but a description—a description, that is, that applies to nothing in the world at all? Why not say, in other words, that there *are* just empirical subjects, ordinary people, some of whom, because of certain very complicated historical-philosophical considerations, have devised this odd, somewhat self-aggrandizing way of describing themselves?[13]

This conception of the subject might seem to accord very well with the non-metaphysical character of transcendental philosophy, on which I have insisted. Affirmation of existence, after all, or the deeper-lying "ontological commitment," belongs to metaphysics, of which transcendental philosophy is the perpetual critique. To say that something exists is always the cue for the critical philosopher, the phenomenologist, to ask questions such as the following: *How* does it exist? What is the meaning of its existence? What are the conditions of the possibility of its having the meaning it does? On our interpretation, transcendental philosophy is not in the business of affirming or denying the existence of anything. Would it not be something like the betrayal of the critical spirit, and its ontological neutrality, to claim that the transcendental subject exists?

Perhaps. But it would equally betray the critical neutrality to declare it a fiction. The concept of fiction is anything but ontologically neutral. To call something a fiction is to say clearly that it does not exist, and in so doing to contrast it with what does exist. This is in effect what Hume was doing when he declared the self a fiction. In the larger context of his religious skepticism, his fictionalism may be seen as an attempt to dispense with the immortal soul as a serious contender for philosophical attention. In somewhat the same spirit, the contemporary materialist D. Dennett seizes on the notion of fiction as a way of dealing with the self as an element of "folk psychology." Whereas Hume begins with the empiricist principle that everything must be traced back to experience, and then reports that he is unable to find the self among his experiences, Dennett begins with the materialist principle that what exists must be "an atom or subatomic particle or . . . other physical item in the world"[14] He then reports, not surprisingly, that the brain contains no such item that we could identify with the self. Initially appearing less dismissive of the notion of the self than is Hume, Dennett finds a place for it by proposing that the brain, like a computer, could generate biographical stories. The central character in these stories are about would be the self. But stories do not have to be about anything real, as we know from novels. The self can be considered a fictional character, just as Sherlock Holmes is a fictional character. In this way Dennett has not only denied the existence of the self by declaring it fictitious, he has also explained this fiction by accounting for its origins, by tracing it to something real, the brain.

The flaw in Dennett's account lies in the notion that brains, conceived as computers, could generate stories. Of course it is quite conceivable that computers could generate printouts that could be read and interpreted as stories, just as participants in a party game, to use another of his examples, can supply random bits of information that can be hilariously combined into stories.[15] But they have to be so combined by someone, just as the printout has to be read and interpreted by someone, in order to become a story. But who is this someone? It is someone with the capacity to read stories and imagine fictional situations. Like a deconstructionist eagerly announcing the death of the author, Dennett finds a way to dispense with the writer and teller of stories. But he cannot dispense with the reader-hearer-interpreter who makes them stories. And this is the very meaning-bestowing conscious self he is trying to explain away. (He also speaks of the self as the "central meaner").[16] Without them the "stories" are nothing but dried ink-marks, or sounding tongues and vocal chords.

Dennett's fictionalism is a valiant attempt at reductionism: instead of reducing the self to a bit of matter, he thinks he has reduced it right out of existence by making it a figment of the imagination. But he seems not to notice that this presupposes the imagination itself, which we might say is consciousness in its most sophisticated form, that is, its intentional or meaning-bestowing relation not only to the existing world, but also to the non-existent, the fictional. When we speak of fiction, we must ask, fiction for whom? Answer: for an existing, meaning-bestowing subject. But could not that subject be fictional as well? Of course, but again: for whom? For a meaning-bestowing subject. Thus we come back to the transcendental self as the always presupposed (i.e., a priori) subject of any awareness, even of itself as an object, even if it tries to "fictionalize" itself.

Existence and Self-Consciousness

These considerations count against the view that the transcendental subject can be considered a mere fiction. In any case, as we have already noted, both Kant and Husserl describe transcendental self-consciousness as a consciousness of my own existence. Kant speaks of it as the "consciousness that I am" (B157), and Husserl describes it as consciousness of the "ego sum" (CM 22). Of course, transcendental reflection has to be more than mere consciousness of existence, since it includes a particular description of the existing subject—namely, *as* the intentional rather than the merely substantial subject. Still, the emphasis on existence in both the Kantian and Husserlian accounts means that in this form of self-awareness I take myself to exist as an intentional subject, rather than, say, merely entertaining the possibility that I *might* exist in this way, or that I might consider myself such even though I know I am not so. This latter would be a genuinely fictive consciousness: imagining or pretending that I am something, knowing all the while that I am not. This is clearly not what Kant and Husserl have in mind.

It is also not quite correct to say that the transcendental subject has a place only in the framework of Kant's and Husserl's elaborate theories. On the contrary, both give us the sense, precisely in their theories of the subject, that they are "discovering" rather than merely "inventing" something. As Husserl says, "as an Ego in the natural attitude, I am likewise and at all times a transcendental Ego, but . . . I know about this only by executing phenomenological reduction" (CM 37). Are they not telling us something important about human existence, rather then merely spinning out the consequences of a very abstract method?

Counting against the view of the transcendental subject as theoretical fiction is the strong suggestion in both authors that the theoretical conception arises out of a pre-theoretical context. For Husserl, indeed, *all* theoretical concepts have their origin in the pre-given life-world. This is a view found not only in the *Crisis* but also in the much earlier *Ideas 2* (ID2 96). If this is so, there must be some reflective experience of the transcendental subject prior to the explicit introduction of the epoche, some pre-theoretical self-awareness on which the phenomenologist can draw as a source of the theoretically refined concept. The self-awareness of intentional experience is described in those sections of *Ideas* 1 and 2 in which he speaks of the intentional act or cogito as an object of potential and actual reflection. "*The essence of the pure Ego . . . includes the possibility of an originary self-grasp, a 'self-perception' "* (ID2 107; see also ID1 78). Statements like this are meant as descriptions of ordinary conscious life, not of the practices of the phenomenologist. Apparently there is some sense in which this kind of self-awareness takes place, at least potentially, prior to the explicit distinction between natural and transcendental reflection, or exists even at the heart of natural reflection itself.

In Kant the same thing is true. As we saw, he introduces the transcendental subject in the context of his theory of the unity of apperception or self-consciousness. It is this unity of apperception that is revealed as the supreme principle of the understanding in the context of the transcendental deduction. But transcendental apperception itself, which we analyzed as the consciousness of self *as* intentional subject or "I think," is not something that occurs only in the philosopher who is engaged in the project of transcendental deduction. "It must be possible for the 'I think' to accompany all my representations" (B131), says Kant. This mode of self-consciousness belongs, then, at least potentially, to experience, not merely to philosophical analysis. While not itself an experience, at least in Kant's sense, transcendental self-consciousness can "accompany," and must at least potentially accompany, all experience. Indeed, as my Kant chapter showed, it is experience itself, and not the transcendental critique of experience, that requires that I be conscious of myself as transcendental subject.

It appears, then, that the subject as transcendental or intentional is something that we have some acquaintance with in everyday, pre-theoretical life, and that the form of reflection in which it is given is not merely a philosophical contrivance. When we begin to think about it in this way, however, the paradoxical character of such reflection becomes all the more obvious.

This paradox was already implicit in my interpretation of Kant. He is engaged in a transcendental analysis of experience or empirical knowledge, in which the natural world becomes accessible to us as an object of scientific cognition. Nature is the realm of events that are governed by relations of strict causality, and in empirical self-consciousness I even take myself to be part of it. But the very experience that gives me access to this realm, and indeed imposes the requirement of strict causality upon it, also requires that I take myself to be spontaneous and intentional, that is, that I take myself to be exempt from the causal requirement and thus not to belong to nature after all.

This duality is of course extremely important for Kant, since it opens the door to freedom and thus serves as the bridge to the full-fledged notion of practical reason in the second Critique. The description of the two forms of self-awareness is clearest in Kant's discussion of the Third Antinomy:

> Man is one of the appearances of the sensible world, and in so far one of the natural causes the causality of which must stand under empirical laws ... Man, however, who knows all the rest of nature solely through the senses, knows himself also through pure apperception; ... He is thus to himself, on the one hand phenomenon, and on the other hand ... a purely intelligible object. (A546f/B574f)

As such an intelligible object, Kant goes on to say, I stand not under laws of nature but under the *ought* of obligation, which in turn requires that I be a free moral agent. It must be pointed out that this passage confirms my claim that pure apperception is anything but empty for Kant, since he presents it here as ascribing definite characteristics— spontaneity as freedom from natural causality—to myself. It is also noteworthy that in this passage, Kant seems to contradict his view that apperception is not a form of self-knowledge. But he is far from suggesting that pure apperception gives me a view of myself that is somehow "truer" than that provided by empirical self-consciousness. Indeed the two forms of self-"knowledge" seem here to be on equal footing, radically different though they are.

In Husserl a similar paradox is obvious: if there is something like a pre-phenomenological awareness of the transcendental subject, then the attitude of transcendental reflection would not be in effect. Still immersed in the natural attitude, with all that it implies about the world and myself as a part of it, I would also somehow be conscious of something—of myself as transcendental subject—that is not worldly at all. In other words, within the natural attitude there would lurk a form of consciousness that would break with the natural attitude without embarking on the full-fledged suspension that constitutes the phenomenological reduction.

Both thinkers, then, seem to postulate a pre-theoretical awareness in which I take myself to be "exempt" or "absent" from the general conditions of worldliness in which I exist. What sort of awareness would this be?

Anxiety, Nothingness and the View from Nowhere

One philosopher who addresses this question explicitly is Jean-Paul Sartre. In his early essay *The Transcendence of the Ego*,[17] Sartre takes up the problem raised in the much-quoted 1933 article by E. Fink, mentioned in chapter 3 (see p. 95). In Husserl, the transcendental subject seems "artificial" because it can be understood only from the point of view of a method that seems unmotivated in the natural attitude. By asserting that there are no motives within the natural attitude for effecting the phenomenological epoche, Fink is in effect claiming that there is no experience prior to the reduction that would give us access to the transcendental subject. The natural standpoint is perfectly coherent as it stands; there are no "cracks" or difficulties that would lead us to question it, much less to suspend it wholesale in the manner recommended by Husserl. Once the epoche is performed, and the role of intentionality is fully grasped, transcendental subjectivity can be understood. But the epoche itself seems like an *acte gratuit*. Husserl describes it as an act of our "perfect freedom"; that is, he stresses that we are free to do it. But do we have a reason to do it?

Sartre agrees with Fink that there are no reasons, no rational motives for the epoche. As Husserl presents it, he says, it appears to be a "miracle" (p. 102). Yet on Sartre's view it is not completely arbitrary. Indeed, it is "imposed on us" from time to time in the form of anxiety or anguish [*angoisse*]. This is the phenomenon Sartre elsewhere calls *nausea*, that emptiness in the pit of the stomach that signals the awareness of the sheer contingency of things in general. He is suggesting that the suspension of the natural attitude first comes to us as an affective break in its hold on us. In the natural attitude we unquestioningly take the world to exist and take ourselves to be part of it.

Anxiety transforms the world into a phenomenon whose ontological status is suspended, and whose meaning-constituted character comes to the fore; as such its meaning is revealed as depending on *me*, or rather on my meaning-bestowing consciousness, not as a thing in the world (for the world is no longer taken for granted), but purely as subject for the world. This vertiginous form of self-awareness, which is not reflection in any ordinary sense at all, is nevertheless the self-awareness of intentional consciousness itself, not as the attribute of a worldly object (i.e., the empirical ego) but as a meaning- and self-constituting process.

Sartre is claiming, then, that Husserl's full-fledged phenomenological method is the explicit articulation and working out of a pre-philosophical, even pre-rational, form of awareness. On this view, "the *epoche* is no longer a miracle, an intellectual method, an erudite procedure: it is an anxiety which is imposed on us and which we cannot avoid: it is both a pure event of transcendental origin and an ever possible accident in our daily life" (p. 103). As anxiety it is more than just a *self*-awareness: like the phenomenological reduction itself it encompasses self and world, as they appear in the natural attitude, and transforms the status of both. Another way of putting it is that in this anxiety the "arbitrary" or "gratuitous" character of the *natural* attitude is revealed. As we saw in the previous chapter (p. 95), Husserl implies this when he claims it is within our "perfect freedom" to suspend the natural attitude. If from within the natural attitude the epoche appears arbitrary, gratuitous, or contrived, and the natural attitude itself quite necessary (this is what "natural" means here), anxiety can suddenly reverse those values. This idea of the transcendental epoche as a reversal or upheaval, an upending of our ordinary way of looking at things, accords well with Kant's and Husserl's claims that they are effecting nothing less than a "revolution" in philosophy. But it has its origin in ordinary—or, rather, extraordinary, but pre-philosophical—experience.

For Sartre, anxiety is more than just an affective intimation of the phenomenological reduction. It is at the same time the consciousness of my radical freedom or spontaneity, a freedom impossible to attribute to the empirical ego that is part of the world. Like Kant, he sees us as alternating between conflicting views of ourselves: on the one hand, as worldly and determined, on the other hand, as transcendental and free. As is well known, the Sartrean approach to ethics is in many ways Kantian: he sees human action not as subjected to rules imposed from without, but as following norms that consciousness imposes on itself.

When he wrote "The Transcendence of the Ego" Sartre was very much under the influence of Husserl. All the same, the point of this short essay was to attack what Sartre thought was a fundamental defect in Husserl's phenomenology, its concept of the transcendental ego. Sartre claims that in speaking of such an ego Husserl was betraying his own best insights, since the phenomenological description of consciousness reveals and requires no such entity. In effect he accuses Husserl of falling prey to a metaphysical prejudice, the view that consciousness needs to be anchored to some underlying substance that holds it together and unifies it. Husserl himself had shown, in his lectures on time-consciousness, according to Sartre, that consciousness unifies itself from within and needs no external, unifying principle. The only valid phenomenological concept of the ego is that of the empirical ego, which is "outside, *in the world*" (p. 31), that is, transcendent, not transcendental. Hence Sartre's title, which also, however, suggests that phenomenology should transcend, or "get beyond," the (transcendental) ego. There is an ego *for* consciousness; *in* or *behind* or *beneath* consciousness, however, "there is no I" [il n'y a pas de *Je*] (p. 48).

Sartre's dispute with Husserl can be seen in retrospect, I think, as a difference over terminology. In light of our own interpretation of Husserl's "theory of the subject" as a non-substantialist one, Sartre's position is in fact entirely consistent with the basic outlines of phenomenology and of transcendental philosophy generally. The same sort of argument, for a "non-egological conception of consciousness," was made by Aron Gurwitsch, another loyal follower of Husserl's.[18] Sartre may have misread, perhaps even deliberately for his own rhetorical purposes, some of Husserl's statements about the ego. In any case his focus in this critique seems to be certain formulations in *Ideas* 1, and Sartre argues against Husserl by pointing out that the substantial ego was found neither in Husserl's earlier work (the lectures *On the Consciousness of Internal Time*) nor his later work (the *Cartesian Meditations*) (*Transcendence of the Ego*, p. 38–39). The term "transcendental ego" can be taken as an expression for just that transcendental unity of consciousness that Sartre admits is essential to it without being in any way substantial. It is this non-egological conception of consciousness, of course, that leads directly to the "phenomenological ontology" presented in Sartre's *Being and Nothingness*.[19] Anguish, as the consciousness of freedom, is at the same time the "apprehension of nothingness" (p. 29). Consciousness, the "for-itself," "must be its own nothingness. The being of consciousness qua consciousness is to exist *at a distance from itself* as a presence to itself, and this empty distance which being carries within itself is Nothingness" (p. 78). Thus Sartre goes beyond asserting merely that "There is no I." His version of the paradox of subjectivity is that the "being of consciousness" is nothingness—*le Néant*.

Historically, I have just traced the improbable transition from the somewhat dry and intellectual rationalism of Husserl to the literary and supposedly irrationalist philosophy of existentialism. The mediating figure in this development is, of course, none other than the early Heidegger, to whom Sartre appeals in introducing anguish as the "apprehension of nothingness." In *Being and Time* and *What Is Metaphysics?* anxiety (*Angst*) is presented as the most fundamental of all dispositions (*Grundbefindlichkeit*). Unlike fear, anxiety has no particular object or situation it seeks to avoid. We know what we fear. Asked what we are anxious about, by contrast, we might say, "nothing in particular." While anxiety has no object, it nevertheless reveals something; what it reveals is *das Nichts* (WM 32–33).

What this means for Heidegger is that in anxiety we no longer are at home in the very place where we are always at home: the world. The world becomes, we could say, meaningless, and in so doing reveals its meaning to us. Its meaning, of course, is its meaning *for us*; what is revealed is thus not just the world but our being in it. Thus, "*that in the face of which one has anxiety [das Wovor der Angst] is Being-in-the-world as such*" (SZ 186). Anxiety reveals, then, in an affective way, exactly what Heidegger's "existential analytic of Dasein" seeks to expose philosophically. To put it in Sartre's Husserlian terms, which of course Heidegger would not use, *Angst* is the prefiguration, from within the natural attitude, of the phenomenological epoche. As we have seen, like Sartre, Heidegger is opposed to the idea of the self as substance: the self is not a thing. It is partly in order to avoid the substance view that he chooses the term *Dasein,* rejecting any terminology involving the "I" or even consciousness. But there is no doubt that *Dasein* plays the role transcendental consciousness does for Husserl and Sartre: it is meaning-bestowing and world-constituting.

If this reading of the post-Husserlian phenomenologists Heidegger and Sartre is correct, they turn out to be much closer to Husserl's (and Kant's) original insights than they made themselves out to be, for all their terminological revisionism and their explicit or implicit criticisms of their predecessors. They belong, in this sense, to the transcendental tradition. At the same time, their talk of "nothingness," as revealed in a kind of pre-theoretical, affective self-awareness, suggests that there is a genuine (transcendental) insight behind the claim of Hume and Dennett that there is something fictional about the self. As part of a strategy for carrying out an empiricist or physicalist reduction, the notion of fiction does not work, as we have seen. But as an expression of the insight that the self is *not a thing,* indeed *no-thing at all,* and above all is not part of the world of things, or indeed part of the world at all, the idea of fiction can be part of a transcendental conception. Hume is making a point against Descartes, and Dennett, like many analytic philosophers, has not progressed much beyond Hume in this respect. The point is a valid one as far as it goes: if the self is not a physical thing, on which everyone agrees, it does not help to make of it a non-physical thing, whatever that would be. The real point is that the transcendental subject is not any kind of thing—it is more like an "absence," or "exemption," as I have called it. But in its paradoxical role as inescapable condition of the possibility of experience, it cannot be denied or argued away.

Paradoxical forms of expression may be unavoidable when trying to articulate philosophically this difficult notion. The existentialists, with their love of paradox, were not the only ones to see this. It is well known that Ludwig Wittgenstein, in his *Tractatus*,[20] sketched a notion of what he called the "philosophical self" [das philosophische Ich] (5.641) or the "metaphysical subject" [metaphysisches Subjekt] (5.633) that can be compared to the transcendental subject of Kant or Husserl. "The philosophical self is not the human being, not the human body, or the human soul, with which psychology deals," he writes (5.641). "The subject does not belong to the world: rather, it is a limit of the world" (5.632). "Where *in* the world is a metaphysical subject to be found?" (5.633). "Thus there really is a sense in which philosophy can talk about the self in a non-psychological way" (5.641). But while we may talk about it, we must also say of this subject, according to Wittgenstein, that "there is no such thing" [Das denkende, vorstellende Subjekt *gibt es nicht*] (5.631, my emphasis).

A similar paradox is expressed in the title of Thomas Nagel's book *The View from Nowhere*. Written in the idiom of contemporary analytic philosophy (as opposed to Wittgenstein's cryptic-aphoristic style), and addressed to its current practitioners, Nagel's book nevertheless raises most of the important issues surrounding transcendental subjectivity and its relation to the empirical subject. "This book is about a single problem," he begins: "how to combine the perspective of a particular person inside the world with an objective view of that same world, the person and his viewpoint included" (p. 3). The modern conception of the objective world, based on physics, powerful as it is, seems incapable of accounting for the very thing that makes it possible: subjective human experience and thought.

First Nagel argues that we should expand our conception of objective reality so as somehow to include the mental within it, even though he is admittedly very vague on how this could be done. But then he concedes that even if it *were* done, something will inevitably be lost. If we try to understand experience from an objective point of view that is distinct from that of the subject of the experience . . . , we will not be able to grasp its most specific qualities unless we can imagine them subjectively. (p. 25)

Pushing the idea of subjectivity to its limit, he arrives at what he calls the "centerless view," or, somewhat misleadingly, the "objective self" (p. 62). Rather than the self objectified, this is the ultimate subject, standing over against the world as a whole. For this subject everything, including its own particular characteristics and point of view, belongs to that world. According to Nagel, his idea of the objective self has "something in common" with Wittgenstein's "metaphysical self" and "a good deal in common" with Husserl's transcendental ego (p. 62n.). Also expressed in this notion, though Nagel does not mention it, is Sartre's idea of consciousness as "distance from itself."

Nagel's book abounds with the same paradoxical metaphors that seem inevitable when dealing with this topic. Central to subjectivity is a point of view, which must be "from somewhere." I am, after all, a particular person, located somewhere, sometime, within the world. But I can become aware of *that*, too. I can keep stepping back from myself. Ultimately the location of this point withdraws into itself and vanishes: it is *nowhere*. Yet it is still a point of view, since it derives its sense from the world, including its own empirical self, which stands before it. Nagel does not speak of *Angst*, but he does mention "the feeling of amazement that is part of the philosophical thought—a strange sense that I both am and am not the hub of the universe" (p. 64). Like Sartre and Heidegger, he does not believe that this sense is something invented or even discovered only by philosophers. "It is a problem that faces every creature with the impulse and the capacity to transcend its particular point of view and to conceive of the world as a whole" (p. 3).

Conclusion

The Paradox of Subjectivity

A s announced, I have in the last few pages added to the "transcendental tradition" a number of philosophers who are not usually
included in it, and would probably not have wanted to be considered
part of it. The issues they discuss, however, are central to that tradition,
and they take up a great many of the ideas of Kant and Husserl,
whether they explicitly say so or not. Above all, they address the problems and paradoxes of the transcendental subject and continue the
discussion of this topic initiated by those philosophers.

Taking their views into account, let me summarize the results.

According to the foregoing account, the transcendental tradition is
not part of the metaphysics of the subject. As inaugurated by Kant, it
is instead a critique of metaphysics in general, and of the metaphysics
of the subject (idealism) in particular. This critique is based on a
broader investigation of the conditions of the possibility—that is to
say, of the general structures—of human experience and knowledge. It
is not the purpose of this investigation to culminate in a metaphysical
doctrine, whether idealistic, realistic, or otherwise. While the early modern turn to subjectivity was motivated by such a purpose, for Kant and
Husserl the transcendental project is carried out under permanent sus-

pension of metaphysical commitments. This is the meaning of what they both call transcendental idealism. The transcendental investigation of experience becomes an end in itself, an ongoing project of reflection and critique. What these philosophers offer us is above all a method for carrying out such reflection, a procedure drawn from the basic concepts of the transcendental unity of apperception or intentionality.

The account of subjectivity that emerges from this critique is the farthest thing from a metaphysical-substance view, contrary to the widespread portrayal of transcendental philosophy by Heidegger and others. The investigation reveals the transcendental subject as a necessary structural feature of human experience; but this subject is revealed not as an underlying substance or *hypokeimenon* that absorbs or overpowers the world by reducing it to its representations, but as a spontaneous and self-related subject of intentionality and meaning. It is the prime condition of the possibility of the world, but only insofar as the world has meaning for us; it does not determine the world's being. Transcendental philosophy recognizes that the world may be more than, and other than, its appearance to us.

The relation between transcendental subject and world is not a part-whole relation but exclusively an intentional relation. Thus the world is not a part of the subject and the subject is not part of the world. But this does not make the transcendental subject worldless, since its only function is to give meaning to the world. It is subject *for* the world, and makes no sense apart from its intentional relation to the world. In this sense its relation to the world is the most intimate of all possible conceptual relations. As we have seen, the transcendental subject is not so much a thing in the world as an absence from it—an absence defined by what it is absent from. It is not a being but that which makes it possible for being to appear. We might say: without the world it would be nothing. But in the world it is also nothing.

Just as the investigation recognizes the transcendental subject—subject for the world—as a necessary part of the structure of experience, so it reveals as equally necessary the empirical subject as object in the world. In addition to the meaning-bond of the intentional relation, which detaches subject from world, the part-whole relation is there as well. The self is indeed a being in the world, one of its constituent parts, bound within it by the inclusion-relations of space, time, and causality. Furthermore, according to our account, these two different senses of the subject, and the distinction between them, are not artifacts of the method of investigation but emerge out of experience itself. Even though something like a transcendental-reflective method is required in order to articulate and clarify this distinction philosophically, it is a distinction that is discovered, not invented. The philosophers of the transcendental tradition are only giving expression to a difference that we are capable of experiencing in our pre- and extra-theoretical life.

These two descriptions of the subject—subject for the world and object in the world—are equally necessary and essentially incompatible. According to the one, I am submerged in the world and constrained by its laws, while according to the other, as conditioning the world's appearance, I am free from those constraints. This is why some have been led to think of transcendental and empirical subjects as if there were really two selves. But manifestly both descriptions refer to the same self. It is just that in reflection I am required to describe myself in radically incompatible ways depending on the framework in which the reflection takes place. For both Kant and Husserl it is self-consciousness, and not just the self, that divides along the trans-cendental-empirical line.

It has been my contention that the transcendental tradition intro-duces us to this radical opposition and provides us with no means for getting beyond it. According to my account, neither of these forms of self-consciousness takes precedence over the other; they are just alter-natives. From the perspective of each, the other appears somehow bizarre, unreal. From that of the natural attitude, the transcendental subject seems artificial, contrived, a mere fiction. From that of the transcendental attitude, the world as a whole, including my (empirical) self within it, looms as "phenomenon," its reality placed in abeyance or suspension. When this happens we feel what the existentialists try to capture by speaking of nausea, vertigo, anxiety, or anguish. It thus leaves us with the paradox that the self is correctly described in incom-patible ways. What are we to make of this paradox?

One might consider it pathological. In a wide-ranging study of the connection between schizophrenia and modern art, literature, and phi-losophy, called *Madness and Modernism*,[1] the psychologist L. Sass devotes his concluding chapter, entitled "Paradoxes of the Reflexive," to what he calls "the strangest and, perhaps, most revealing of the many par-adoxes that lie coiled at the heart of the schizophrenic condition" (p. 324). This is the tendency of many schizophrenics to alternate be-tween feelings of "omnipotence and passivity, of omniscience and utter ignorance" (p. 326). On the one hand, they feel "poised at the epicenter of the universe" ("my thoughts can influence things"; "to keep the world going, I must not stop thinking";); on the other hand, they have "feelings of persecution, powerlessness and inferiority: the same patient who declares himself to be omnipotent will also say that he doesn't exist, or that his body or his thoughts are under alien control" (p. 325).

Sass then compares this conflicted mental state with the opposition between the transcendental and the empirical self that begins with Kant. "If the world is dependent on consciousness rather than vice versa," he writes, alluding to Kant's Copernican revolution, then consciousness must be "a free spontaneity, operating in a self-generated sphere of total freedom." But in addition to being the "ultimate subjective center, the constitutor of the All (or at least of all that *we* can know), consciousness beginning with Kant also became a prime *object* of study . . ." (p. 328). Thus the self was placed in the "empirical order of objectifiable entities, and this conflicted with its status as a *transcendental* being to which and for which all entities must appear" (p. 329).

There is no doubt that the comparison, as Sass presents it, is somehow apt. The question is how to interpret it. Sass himself is understandably and laudably cautious about the overall significance of this and the many other fascinating parallels he draws between schizophrenia and modern thought. He denies looking for causal connections. (The most obvious one, that one can be driven insane by reading the *Critique of Pure Reason*, may be true but would probably not account for very many cases of schizophrenia.) Instead he seeks "illuminating analogies," "affinities rather than influences" (p. 9). "Hyperreflexivity" (p. 8) is one of his key terms of comparison. His intent, he says, is neither to "denigrate modernism" by simply saying that it *is* schizophrenic, nor to "glorify schizophrenic forms of madness" as examples of creative thought (p. 9). Applied to philosophy, the one extreme would be to say that the philosophers of the transcendental tradition are themselves mad; the other would be to romanticize the schizophrenic as one whose madness contains a deep philosophical insight. But there may be some truth in both these extremes; or so it will seem to those both inside and outside the discipline who think that there is a thin line between madness and philosophy.

The fact is, however, that most philosophers have found the paradox of subjectivity intolerable. The philosophical temperament has always favored the one over the many, concord over opposition, and will often find it even when it is not there. One of the great achievements of the *Critique of Pure Reason* is its portrayal of the almost irresistible demand of human reason to pass beyond the conditions and incongruities of experience in order to find repose in the unity and coherence of the unconditioned. There is plenty of evidence that this demand was acutely felt by Kant and Husserl as well. In his writings on morality, teleology, and religion, Kant gives expression to his yearning for the worldview of Christian natural theology. And Husserl often speaks as the absolute idealist he would like to be. It might be thought that these philosophers overcome the transcendental-empirical conflict by appealing to the appearance-reality distinction. Kant, after all, locates the empirical self in the world of appearances, just as Husserl locates it in the "bracketed" world of the natural attitude. But Kant's theory does not permit him to claim the reality "in itself" of the spontaneous, transcendental subject. And for Husserl the world of the natural attitude is not metaphysically downgraded to the status of mere appearance, it is simply bracketed. Both philosophers recognized, I think, that their transcendental procedure did not authorize the transition to metaphysical claims. As I argued in the last chapter, commentators, both sympathetic and hostile, cannot imagine being content just to articulate this incompatible alternative, and so they push Kant and Husserl in the direction of metaphysical idealism. But in doing so they miss their most important insight.

One reaction to the position I am attributing to the transcendental tradition is to characterize it simply as dualism, a reaffirmation of Cartesianism. But the transcendental-empirical distinction is by no means equivalent to the mind-body distinction. More importantly, the transcendental philosophers hesitate between two incompatible descriptions of self and world. Dualism is a metaphysical doctrine that straightforwardly affirms the existence of mental and extended substance. It thus overcomes the hesitation by enshrining ontologically the two kinds of substance. Then it seeks to satisfy the philosophical urge for unity by explaining how the two substances interact, a notoriously futile effort. To call transcendental philosophy dualism would be to make the mistake, discussed in the last chapter, of thinking that transcendental idealism is some third metaphysical doctrine between realism and idealism. Instead, as I argued there, it is not a metaphysical doctrine at all but a method of reflection, what today is called a "research program." What it reveals is a paradoxical situation that philosophers feel inclined to try to resolve metaphysically. One could say that Descartes was already aware of the paradox, and that metaphysical dualism was his attempt to resolve it. But as we have seen, transcendental philosophy, as a critique of metaphysics, is as much directed at dualism as at other metaphysical doctrines.

The more common route, of course, has been the attempt to eliminate one or the other of the two sides. The earliest reaction to Kant was that of German Idealism, which begins with Fichte. This philosopher claims to be doing nothing but rethinking Kant. And he comes close to the Kantian spirit in the first introduction to the *Wissenschaftslehre* (1797) when he speaks of "idealism" and "dogmatism" as two opposed "systems," neither of which can refute the other. "What sort of philosophy one chooses," he writes of these two alternatives, "depends, therefore, on what sort of man one is."[2] This much-quoted phrase expresses well the Kantian ideas of the antinomy of pure reason and the primacy of the practical, where the only resolution to the paradox is practical rather than theoretical. But Fichte disregards his own precepts, going on to argue copiously for the truth of idealism as a "system," and making the primacy of the practical into a metaphysical claim about the subject.

A more common reaction in our own day to the transcendental paradox is the attempt on the part of some post-positivists to eliminate subjectivity altogether in some form of materialist reduction. In chapter 4 I discussed briefly one of the most interesting, not to say fanciful, of these attempts, that of Dennett (pp. 123f.) The common characteristic of those who undertake such a project, at least to the transcendental philosopher-phenomenologist, is that in order to preserve their a priori commitment to a materialist ontology they are required to deny the existence of something that literally stares them in the face. In this they resemble nothing so much as theologians trying to argue evil out of a world of whose uniform goodness they are convinced in advance. What stares them in the face is not only the qualitative difference between consciousness and the third-person processes of the brain and nervous system, but also the fact that subjectivity and intentionality are the always presupposed conditions of the possibility of the scientific investigations on which their philosophical conclusions so heavily depend.

Discomfort with the transcendental-empirical paradox can likewise be discerned at the roots of some of the most important developments in post-structuralist thought. Foucault expresses it in the famous chapter in *The Order of Things* entitled "Man and his Doubles."[3] "The threshold of our modernity," he writes, is marked by "the constitution of an empirico-transcendental doublet which is called *man*" (p. 319). What this means is that man "is at the same time at the foundation of all positivities and present, in a way that cannot even be termed privileged, in the element of empirical things" (p. 344). Foucault ventures the conjecture, which sounds very much like a hope, that this conception of man will disappear altogether. Adopting the apocalyptic tone of the late Heidegger, Foucault suggests that this disappearance would depend on "some event of which we can at the moment do no more than sense the possibility—without knowing either what its form will be or what it promises" (p. 387).

Similarly apocalyptic sentiments are expressed in some of Jacques Derrida's early essays, particularly one whose title echoes Foucault's conjecture: "The Ends of Man."[4] Derrida is of course playing on several of the senses of "end," as does Heidegger when he speaks of the end of philosophy. Significant for my topic is that this essay is an extended reflection on the distinction between empirical and transcendental subjectivity, or more broadly between the empirical sense of man and the philosophical sense of subjectivity articulated by Hegel, Husserl, and Heidegger. Derrida's critical point is that while all three thinkers abjure anything like psychologism, philosophical anthropology, or "humanism," none succeeds entirely in getting beyond psychological, anthropological, or empirical considerations. Hence they remain in the thrall of an unresolved polarity of the empirical and the transcendental, and this is what has brought contemporary French philosophy to the point of "total trembling" (p. 134).

Even French phenomenology was not on the whole very comfortable with the distinction between transcendental and empirical subjectivity. The work of Merleau-Ponty and Ricoeur can be described as attempting, in somewhat different ways, to qualify, if not completely to overcome, this distinction. The former insists on the bodily character of subjectivity and the subjective character of the body. The latter emphasizes the dependence of subjectivity on language and interpretation. Both dwell on the embeddedness of subjectivity in society and history, and both want to take the Freudian unconscious seriously. But these important innovations count against the transcendental-empirical distinction only if transcendental subjectivity and intentionality are associated exclusively with consciousness understood in the narrowest sense. What characterizes the transcendental, according to our account, is its meaning-bestowing and world-constituting capacity. Why should this capacity not be exercised through the body and through language, even in an unconscious manner, by a socially and historically embedded subject? Nothing in the transcendental tradition, as it has been interpreted here, requires that subjectivity be disembodied or separated from language, society, and history. Merleau-Ponty's and Ricoeur's works are critical not so much of transcendental phenomenology as of traditional metaphysical dualism. If they claim to find traces of this doctrine in Husserl and Kant, they are, I think, mistaken. But in any case their aim, in contrast to that of most critics of transcendental philosophy, is not to unite oppositions in a unified metaphysics but to pursue and enrich the phenomenological program.

Phenomenological displeasure with the transcendental-empirical distinction really goes back to the early work of Heidegger. His reaction too can be traced to his tendency, noted in chapter 1, to misread Kant and Husserl, even in *Being and Time*, as inheritors of the Cartesian substantialization of the subject. Yet the transcendental-empirical distinction is recognized, though in different terminological guise, in that very work. *Dasein* is meaning-bestowing, world-constituting intentionality, and the basic disposition of *Angst* permits us to be aware of this. But most of the time we think of ourselves as just another thing in the world (i.e., as *vorhanden*), as just anybody (*das Man*), subject to laws and meanings determined anonymously, inauthentically. Like Kant and Husserl, Heidegger in this work essentially leaves us suspended between these two incompatible views of ourselves, as if the alteration between them were simply and descriptively an inescapable part of human experience.

Thus the early Heidegger really belongs, as we suggested in chapter 4 (p. 130), to the transcendental tradition. What he attacks, both in *Being and Time* and later, is not really the transcendental view at all but metaphysical idealism. The trajectory he traces in his later work, from Descartes through Leibniz to Fichte and Hegel, is the history of those philosophers who, unwilling to accept the paradox of subjectivity, reduce the world to representation.

This brings us back to the point at which we began—Heidegger's reading of the history of modern philosophy, and the attacks on the "metaphysics of the subject" that arise out of it. Heidegger and his post-modern successors, who see in this historical trajectory the progress of the will to power, make a valid point. Especially valuable is the insight that scientific realism, with its implicit links to technology, instead of being opposed to metaphysical idealism, is just the reverse side of this same conception. Unfortunately, the transcendental philosophers have been absorbed into this trajectory, and in a sense the baby has been thrown out with the bathwater: what is distinctive about the transcendental conception of subjectivity and its difference from the modern idealist tradition have been lost. Lost as well is the *critique* of metaphysics of the subject—a much more subtle and devastating critique than the one put forward by Heidegger—contained in the transcendental tradition.

But the most serious consequence of the recent attack on the metaphysics of the subject, inspired by Heidegger, is the neglect by philosophers of subjectivity itself as a central philosophical topic. This is what Kant, Husserl, and the other philosophers of the transcendental tradition have tried to elucidate, in all its paradoxical complexity and richness. In the foregoing pages I have tried to describe how they have gone about this and to reawaken an appreciation for their great accomplishment.

Notes

Introduction: Reviving the Question of Subjectivity

1. Jürgen Habermas, *The Philosophical Discourse of Modernity*, tr. Frederick Lawrence (Cambridge: MIT Press, 1987), p. 294 and *passim*.

2. See John Searle, *Intentionality* (Cambridge: Cambridge University Press, 1983), and *The Rediscovery of the Mind* (Cambridge: MIT Press, 1992); Thomas Nagel, "What Is It Like to Be a Bat?" in *Mortal Questions* (Cambridge: Cambridge University Press, 1979), pp. 165 ff.; *The View from Nowhere* (New York: Oxford University Press, 1986).

3. In Germany the work of Manfred Frank is especially to be noted; see his *Selbstbewußtsein und Selbsterkenntnis* (Stuttgart: Philipp Reclam jun., 1991). Conferences of German and American scholars, including Frank, have given rise to two excellent collections: *The Modern Subject: Conceptions of the Self in Classical German Philosophy* (Albany: SUNY Press, 1995) and *Figuring the Self: Subject, Absolute and Others in Classical German Philosophy* (Albany: SUNY Press, 1997). In France see the work of Luc Ferry and Alain Renaut, especially in this regard Renaut's *L'ère de l'individu* (Paris: Gallimard, 1989).

4. See Jean-Luc Nancy's introduction to *Who Comes after the Subject?*, ed. E. Cadava, P. Connor, and J.-L. Nancy (New York: Routledge, 1991), p. 4

5. On the role of Heidegger in French philosophy see Luc Ferry and Alain Renaut, *Heidegger et les modernes* (Paris: Bernard Grasset, 1988).

6. Alasdair MacIntyre, "Relativism, Power and Philosophy," in *After Philosophy*, ed. K. Baynes, J. Bohman, T. McCarthy (Cambridge: MIT Press, 1987), p. 385.

7. See Gilbert Ryle, *The Concept of Mind* (New York: Barnes and Noble, 1949) p. 15; Daniel Dennett, *Consciousness Explained* (Boston: Little, Brown, 1991), pp. 101ff.

Chapter One

1. Because of the wide variety and, in some cases, unreliability of Heidegger translations, I have decided to provide my own translations, referring always to the German originals. In most cases I have provided the German text I am translating.

2. See Fernand Braudel, *Ecrits sur l'histoire* (Paris: Flammarion, 1969).

3. See also FD 77 and K 13f.

4. See EP 65: the sciences bear the certification of their birth from philosophy [die Urkunde ihrer Geburt aus der Philosophie].

5. See also *Logik. Die Frage nach der Wahrheit*, ed. P. Jaeger, 1977; and *Phänomenologische Interpretationen von Kants Kritik der reinen Vernunft*, ed. I. Görland, 1977; both Frankfurt/M: Vittorio Klostermann. Heidegger Gesamtausgabe, vols. 21 and 25, respectively.

Chapter Two

A shorter version of this chapter appeared under the same title in *Transcendental Philosophy and Everyday Experience*, ed. T. Rockmore and V. Zeman (Highlands: Humanities Press, 1997) pp. 96–110.

1. I follow the standard practice of referring to the pages of the Academy Edition. These are given in both the English and the German versions on which I draw: Immanuel Kant, *Kritik der reinen Vernunft*, ed. R. Schmidt (Hamburg: Felix Meiner Verlag, 1956); and *Immanuel Kant's Critique of Pure Reason*, tr. N. Kemp Smith (London: McMillan, 1963).

2. *Grundlegung zur Meaphysik der Sitten*, ed. K. Vorländer (Hamburg: Felix Mainer Verlag, 1957) p. 4.

3. See Karl Ameriks's discussion of the various alternatives at the beginning of his "Kant's Transcendental Deduction as a Regressive Argument" (*Kant-Studien*, 69 [1978], 273ff.) and in the second part of his "Recent Work on Kant's Theoretical Philosophy" (*American Philosophical Quarterly*, 19 [1982], 1–24.)

4. Some commentators, of course, hold that this is precisely what is to be proved. Ameriks ("Kant's Transcendental Deduction") has, in my view, successfully argued against this interpretation as found, e.g., in the work of P. F. Strawson, J. Bennett, and R. P. Wolff. I shall have more to say about this later.

5. Kant uses the expression "transcendental subject" at A346/B404.

6. See Manfred Frank, *Selbstbewußtsein und Selbsterkenntnis* (Stuttgart: Reklam, 1991), pp. 24ff.

7. See Dieter Sturma, *Kant über Selbstbewußtsein* (Hildesheim: Georg Olms, 1985), pp. 23ff.

8. Rudolf A. Makkreel, *Imagination and Interpretation in Kant* (Chicago: University of Chicago Press, 1990), pp. 103ff. I shall come back to Makkreel's proposal later.

9. Manfred Frank, *Selbstbewußtstein*, pp. 14ff.

10. Cf. Joseph Claude Evans, Jr.: *The Metaphysics of Transcendental Subjectivity: Descartes, Kant and W. Sellars* (Amsterdam: B. R. Grüner, 1984), pp. 73f.

11. John Locke, *An Essay concerning Human Understanding* (Chicago: Henry Regnery Co., 1956), p. 17.

12. It is interesting to note that two "phenomenological" commentators come to opposite conclusions on this point. R. Aquila, in *Representational Mind* (Bloomington: Indiana University Press, 1983), claims that intentionality is already present in sense representations, whereas A. Gurwitsch, in *Kants Theorie des Verstandes* (ed. T. Seebohm. Dordrecht: Kluwer, 1990, pp. 123ff.) claims that because Kant never distinguishes between sensations and the sensible properties of objects, he never arrives at a proper understanding of intentionality at all. An intermediate position is attempted by Evans (*Metaphysics*, pp. 52ff.). My own attempt is closer to that of G. Prauss in his *Erscheinung bei Kant* (Berlin: deGruyter, 1971).

13. This is what Henry Allison calls the reciprocity thesis, the "reciprocal connection between the transcendental unity of apperception and the representation of objects." H. Allison, *Kant's Transcendental Idealism* (New Haven: Yale University Press, 1983), p. 144.

14. *Logical Investigations* (tr. J. N. Findlay [New York: Humanities Press, 1970], vol. 2, p. 576). The word content (*Inhalt*) seems ill chosen for Husserl's purposes, when used in its intentional sense, but this use of it is already found in Brentano before him. Unfortunately, this use has been perpetuated by such contemporary philosophers as D. Dennett (cf. *Content and Consciousness* [London: Routledge and Kegan Paul, 1969]).

15. "In the essence of the mental process itself lies not only *that* it is consciousness but also *whereof* it is consciousness..." ID1 74.

16. H. Allison, "Kant's Refutation of Materialism," in *The Monist* (vol. 72, no. 2, 1989), p. 202. I have emphasized the words "consider ourselves" to underline that this is the manner in which we are conscious of ourselves in this mode of self-consciousness.

17. See A216/B263 and A418/B446 and n. In the latter passage Kant also uses the term "world."

18. See note 4.

19. See Henry Allison, *Kant's Transcendental Idealism*, pp. 14–34.

20. Rudolf Makkreel, *Imagination and Interpretation in Kant*.

21. Immanuel Kant, *Prolegomena to Any Future Metaphysics* [etc.], tr. Paul Carus, rev. J. W. Ellington (Indianapolis: Hackett, 1977), p. 75n. Emphasis added.

22. A further advantage, for Makkreel's purposes and also our own later on, is the discovery of a non-vitalist conception of "life" in Kant that foreshadows the use of this term by Dilthey and Husserl.

23. Cf. Evans, *Metaphysics*, p. 74.

24. *Prolegomena* [etc.], p. 48.

25. J. G. Fichte, *Science of Knowledge*, ed. and tr. P. Heath and J. Lachs (Cambridge: Cambridge University Press, 1982). See *Fichtes Werke*, ed. I. H. Fichte (Berlin: de Gruyter, 1971).

26. G. W. F. Hegel, *Phänomenologie des Geistes*, ed. J. Hoffmeister (Hamburg: Felix Meiner, 6th ed., 1952), p. 70. My translation.

27. *A Treatise of Human Nature*, ed. L. A. Selby-Bigge (Oxford: Clarendon Press, 1965), p. 254.

28. Daniel Dennett, "Why Everyone Is a Novelist," *Times Literary Supplement*, September 1988, p. 17. See also Dennett's *Consciousness Explained* (Boston: Little, Brown, 1991), pp. 410ff.

29. See Henry Allison's discussion in *Kant's Transcendental Idealism*, pp. 310ff. and in his "Kant's Refutation of Materialism," p. 190.

30. See the first part of Ameriks's "Recent Work" for a discussion of the debate on this issue.

31. See Gerold Prauss, *Kant und das Problem der Dinge an sich* (Bonn: Bouvier, 1974), and Henry Allison, *Kant's Transcendental Idealism*.

32. R. C. S. Walker, *Kant* (London: Routledge and Kegan Paul, 1978), p. 122

33. Allison, "Kant's Refutation," p. 202.

34. Quoted by Heidegger in K, pp. 187f.

35. "was er als freihandelndes Wesen aus sich selber macht, oder machen kann und soll." *Anthropologie in pragmatischer Hinsicht* (Berlin: de Gruyter, 1968), p. 119.

Chapter Three

1. Here I am using and referring to the English translation.

2. I am following Findlay in this translation. This term, which seems to have come into currency in the nineteenth century, must be distinguished from *Erfahrung*, also usually translated as "experience," which is the older term and the central one for Kant. See the discussion of this term on p. 70.

3. Husserl quotes from Brentano's *Psychologie vom empirischen Standpunkt* (Leipzig: Duncker & Humblot, 1911), vol. 1, p. 115.

4. Husserl had already attacked a version of this theory in Investigation 1, section 23. His most extensive account is in *Ideas 2*, section 43.

5. It is this assumption that serves as the starting point of Jacques Derrida's critique in *Speech and Phenomena*, tr. D. Allison (Evanston: Northwestern University Press, 1973).

6. On the different ways to the reduction, see Iso Kern, "The Three Ways to the Transcendental Phenomenological Reduction," in *Husserl: Expositions and Appraisals*, ed. F. Elliston and P. McCormick (Notre Dame: University of Notre Dame Press, 1977), pp. 126ff. See also R. Bernet, I. Kern, and E. Marbach, *An Introduction to Husserlian Phenomenology* (Evanston: Northwestern University Press, 1993), pp. 65ff.

7. What Husserl sometimes calls the formal region, that of formal logic and formal ontology, is not properly a region "but the empty form of any region whatever" (ID1 21).

8. See R. Bernet et al., *An Introduction to Husserlian Phenomenology*, pp. 26ff.

9. Eugen Fink, *Studien zur Phänomenologie, 1930–1939* (The Hague: M. Nijhoff, 1966), pp. 110f.

10. See R. Bernet et al. *An Introduction to Husserlian Phenomenology*, pp. 60ff.

11. The case for the non-foundational character of Husserl's phenomenology has recently been made by two commentators: Dagfin Follesdal, "The Justification of Logic and Mathematics in Husserl's phenomenology," in *Phenomenology and the Formal Sciences*, ed. T. Seebohm, D. Follesdal, and J. Mohanty (Dordrecht: Kluwer, 1991), p. 25 and *passim*; and John Drummond, *Husserlian Intentionality and Non-Foundational Realism* (Dordrecht: Kluwer, 1990). For a sophisticated defense of a foundationalist account of Husserl's phenomenology see J. N. Mohanty, *Transcendental Phenomenology: An Analytic Account* (Oxford: Basil Blackwell, 1989), pp. 115ff.

12. Paul Ricoeur (in his *Husserl* [Evanston: Northwestern University Press, 1967], p.36) makes a strong distinction between "a methodological rather than a doctrinal idealism." See also Gerhard Funke, *Phänomenologie: Metaphysik oder Methode?* (Bonn: Bouvier Verlag Herbert Grundmann, 1979).

Chapter Four

1. See, for example, Thomas Seebohm, *Die Bedingungen der Möglichkeit der Transzendental-Philosophie* (Bonn: H. Bouvier, 1962); and Iso Kern, *Husserl und Kant* (The Hague: M. Nijhoff, 1964). J. N. Mohanty has written on this connection in many of his writings, most recently in "Kant and Husserl" (*Husserl Studies* 13, no. 1, 1996, 19–30).

2. "Kant und die Idee der Transzendentalphilosophie," in *Erste Philosophie* vol. 1, ed. R. Boehm (Husserliana 7, The Hague: M. Nijhoff, 1956), pp. 230ff.

3. See Chapter 2, note 1 on references to Kant.

4. See chapter 2, note 2, and CM 156.

5. See Kant, *Prolegomena to Any Future Metaphysics* [etc.], tr. Paul Carus, rev. J. W. Ellington (Indianapolis: Hackett, 1977), p. 113n.

6. "Hegels Begriff der Erfahrung," in *Holzwege* (Frankfurt am Main: Vittorio Klostermann, 1957). Two volumes of the Heidegger *Gesamtausgabe* (Frankfurt am Main: V. Klostermann) are devoted to Hegel: vol. 32, *Hegels Phänomenologie des Geistes*, ed. I. Görland, 1980, and vol. 68, *Hegel*, ed. I. Schüßler, 1993.

7. Allison, *Kant's Transcendental Idealism* (New Haven: Yale University Press, 1983), p. 26

8. This is essentially the view put forward by John Drummond in *Husserlian Intenationality and Non-Foundational Realism* (Dordrecht: Kluwer, 1990).

9. Paul Ricoeur, *Husserl* (Evanston: Northwestern University Press, 1967), p. 36.

10. See Gerhard Funke, *Phänomenologie: Metaphysik oder Methode?* (Bonn: Bouvier Verlag Herbert Grundmann, 1979).

11. See also Thomas Nagel, *The View from Nowhere* (New York: Oxford University Press, 1986), pp. 9, 26.

12. Jacques Derrida, *Speech and Phenomena*, tr. D. Allison (Evanston: Northwestern University Press, 1973), p. 4.

13. I proposed this idea in response to the work of J. N. Mohanty in a paper entitled "Mohanty on Transcendental Philosophy" (in *Phenomenology: East and West*, ed. F. Kirkland and D. P. Chattopadhyaya [Dordrecht: Kluwer, 1993] pp. 1–11.) Mohanty has responded in the same volume (pp. 269ff.) and also in "Transcendental Philosophy and the Life-World" (in *Transcendental Philosophy and Everyday Experience*, ed. T. Rockmore and V. Zeman [Atlantic Highlands, N.J.: Humanities, 1997], pp. 33ff.).

14. Daniel Dennett, "Why Everyone Is a Novelist," *Times Literary Supplement*, September 1988, p. 17

15. See Daniel Dennett, *Consciousness Explained* (Boston: Little, Brown, 1991), p. 10.

16. Ibid., p. 228.

17. Tr. F. Williams and R. Kirkpatrick (New York: Hill and Wang, 1993).

18. "A Non-Egological Conception of Consciousness," in his *Studies in Phenomenology and Psychology* (Evanston: Northwestern University Press, 1966).

19. Tr. Hazel E. Barnes (New York: Philosophical Library, 1956).

20. *Tractatus Logico-Philosophicus,* tr. D. F. Pears and B. F. McGuiness (London: Routledge & Kegan Paul, 1963).

Conclusion: The Paradox of Subjectivity

1. Louis A. Sass, *Madness and Modernism* (New York: Basic Books, 1992).

2. J. G. Fichte, *The Science of Knowledge,* ed. and tr. P. Heath and J. Lachs (Cambridge: Cambridge University Press, 1988), p. 16.

3. Michel Foucault, *The Order of Things* (New York: Vintage Books, 1973), pp. 303ff.

4. In *Margins of Philosophy*, tr. Alan Bass (Chicago: University of Chicago Press, 1982), pp. 109ff.

Index

Adorno, Theodor, 3
Allison, Henry, 44, 59, 61, 108–09
Ameriks, Karl, 142, 144
analytic philosophy, 4, 7, 131
ancient philosophy, 14–15, 22
Annales school, 13
anthropology, 5
   philosophical, 62
anxiety, 127–30, 135
apodicticity, 82
apperception, transcendental and
   empirical, 36–39, 42–44, 52, 105–
   07, 125
a priori, 35, 42, 48, 57, 62, 80, 104
Aquila, Richard, 143
Aristotle, 11, 16
attitude,
   natural, 77, 82–85, 88, 96, 110–12,
     126–27, 135
   naturalistic, 83

personalistic, 83
phenomenological, 110, 112, 118
Augustine, 76
Averroes, 53–54

being,
   of beings, 13, 30, 103
   question of, 12
Bennett, Jonathan, 142
Berkeley, George, 104, 108
Bernet, Rudolf, 144
bracketing, 78, 109, 120
Braudel, Fernand, 142
Brentano, Franz, 70

Carr, David, 54
Cassirer, Ernst, 27
categorial intuition, 26, 29
categories, 41–45